March 27th 1943 saw one of the biggest catastrophes in British naval history as the converted aircraft carrier HMS *Dasher* blew up and sank in the Firth of Clyde. The World War II loss of 379 lives was second only in home waters to the *Royal Oak*.

Yet mystery surrounded the circumstances of this tragedy and until this book appeared many of the survivors and the bereaved relatives of casualties had no idea what had happened. Shrouded in wartime secrecy the most basic facts about trauma, injury and death were not known.

Authors John and Noreen Steele have gleaned further testimonies and facts since first publication and in this new edition *Dasher* has given up more of her secrets. Seabed surveys and contacts from friends and survivors have yielded both the horror of war and information about the circumstances of the explosion and sinking of a strategically important vessel. An amazing connection has been established also with **The Man Who Never Was** – the Allied ruse to deceive the Germans about the likely point of mainland Europe invasion. It seems certain from evidence presented in these pages that the body used was a *Dasher* casualty, named for the first time in this new edition.

The Secrets
of HMS *DASHER*

John Steele & Noreen Steele

Argyll
publishing

First Published 1995, Reprinted 1996
2nd edition 1997, 3rd edition 2002
Argyll Publishing
Glendaruel
Argyll PA22 3AE
Scotland
www.argyllpublishing.com

**British Library Cataloguing-in-Publication
Data.**
**A catalogue record for this book is available
from the British Library.**

ISBN 1 902831 39 X

Typeset & Origination
Cordfall Ltd, Glasgow

Printing
Bell & Bain Ltd, Glasgow

This book is dedicated
to the 379 officers and men who
perished when HMS *Dasher*
sank on 27th March 1943
and to all those who were left to mourn.
'We will remember them'

HMS Dasher – aircraft carrier of the World War II era

ACKNOWLEDGEMENTS

For their help in compiling this memorial book we wish to record our thanks to the following: the survivors who shared their memories; the bereaved families who shared painful memories and allowed us to use precious photographs; Tony Barr, Ardrossan; Rt Rev Msgnr John Barry, North Berwick; Horst Bredow, U-Boot Archiv, Cuxhaven; Alex Buchanan, Motherwell; Caledonian MacBrayne; Commonwealth War Graves Commission, Maidenhead; the Cabinet Office, London; Herbert Geoffrey Cameron, Spain; Jesus Copeiro, Huelva, Spain; the late Captain AP Culmer DSC & BAR RN; Ian Douglas, Racks Village; HM Coastguard, Greenock; Fleet Air Arm Museum; General Register Office for Scotland; Colin Gibbon, Pontypridd, for first putting forward the connection between *Dasher* and The Man Who Never Was and for access to his copious research; Bill Haggerty, Ayr; David Hendry, Largs; Hydrographic Office, London; Peter Jordan; Dipl. Ing. Karl-Werner & Maria Fischer, Kassel; Barbara Kay, Ayr; John Linton; Ministry of Defence Secretariat (Naval Staff) and Naval Historical Branch, London; the late Captain Archie Murchie, Ardrossan; North Ayrshire Council; Brian A Philpott, Grange-over-Sands; Public Records Office, Kew; Saltcoats Library; Sunshine Radio, Nerja, Spain; Denise Richardson MA; Paul Stevenston, Funeral Director, Saltcoats; Terry Whippy, Eastbourne; and Brian Wilson MP.

John Steele & Noreen Steele
Ardrossan June 2004

Flying on and off Dasher *was by no means an exact science as this picture of a 'pranged' Swordfish of 891 Squadron shows – note the bent propeller blades*

CONTENTS

Some of the **Dasher** *crew pose for the photographer in New York, 1942*

FOREWORD

to the first paperback edition

This is the third time I have written a foreword to a version of the book by John and Noreen Steele about the fate of HMS *Dasher*. That reflects the fact that this is a story which, having been suppressed for so long, continues to grow and grow. The Steeles are correspondingly assiduous in their commitment and researches.

The story of HMS *Dasher* is, by any standards, extraordinary. Her sinking stands as second only to the *Ark Royal* in the league table of British naval disasters which occurred in home waters during Wolrd War II. Yet it remained a virtual secret for several decades – a mass sacrifice by men of the Royal Navy which many preferred not to talk about.

Even the announcement of the *Dasher*'s loss, in *The Times* of London, came a full two years after the event and was conveyed in the tiniest of print. It was not good for British morale, at home or abroad, to advertise an avoidable tragedy which had not even occurred at the hands of the enemy.

The whole process, to which the Steeles have given sustained leadership, of finally recognising the sacrifices of those who lost their lives on board HMS *Dasher* has been immensely appreciated. This applies both to the families of the victims and also to the survivors who must have wondered if the loss of their comrades was ever going to be properly recognised.

However, it is impossible to release such a tale without sparking the interest of others or, indeed, encountering cross-currents of work which have been going on elsewhere. Thus, as a fascinating appendix to the story of HMS *Dasher*, we now have a plausible theory about how it tied in with the celebrated story of The Man Who Never Was.

It is a matter of well-recorded history that a body was placed from a British submarine in the waters off the south of Spain in May 1943. This was the centrepiece of a brilliantly successful operation to mislead the Germans into believing that the Allied landings to clear the Axis forces out of Southern Europe would be focused on Greece and not Sicily.

The body had been given a name and an identity in order to equip it with the credibility which would be necessary to persuade the Germans that this had been someone qualified to carry the vital messages contained in the accompanying briefcase. These were the decoy plans which diverted the Nazi effort toward Greece and thus saved thousands of Allied lives.

For students of this classic tale, the true identity of The Man Who Never Was has long been a source of fascination. This account opens up the strong possibility that one of the bodies from HMS *Dasher* occupied that crucial, if posthumous, role. It is an ingenious piece of detective work on the part of the Steeles and their collaborators.

The story of HMS *Dasher* has long been familiar to many on the Clyde Coast, particularly in Ardrossan and on the Isle of Arran. It was from these communities that the rescue efforts and care for survivors came, and it was on these shores that the wreckage was washed up in the months that followed the explosion and sinking. Since 1993 there has been a fine memorial in Ardrossan to those who perished.

Above all, the story of HMS *Dasher* is about people and much of it is told in the words of those who were involved, including some from the small number of survivors. It is a reminder of how, in time of war, there are precious few rights even for the bereaved. John and Noreen Steele have performed their own heroic task in reviving the forgotten tale of HMS *Dasher* and in respecting the memory of the hundreds who went with her to the depth of the Firth of Clyde.

Brian Wilson MP

JUNE 2002

PREFACE

At twenty minutes to five in the afternoon of March 27th, 1943,
HMS *Dasher*, an American-built aircraft carrier, blew up in the Clyde
estuary and sank within eight minutes. Three hundred and seventy
nine young men lost their lives. Twenty three bodies were identified
and the relatives were informed of their loss and of the Royal Navy
funeral arrangements. No mention was made that three quarters of
the crew had perished, nor that the ship was gone.

As for the remaining three hundred and fifty six families, they
were left with no information whatsoever. Their loved ones were
reported as 'missing'. No details were ever to be forthcoming. They
were never to be informed of where their loved ones lost their lives
or what had happened to the aircraft carrier.

Many people in and around Ardrossan, Ayrshire were involved
in one way or another with Britain's second biggest catastrophe in
home waters during World War II. These people had either
witnessed the terrible sea tragedy or they had assisted in the rescue
operation.

Three hundred and fifty six parents, wives, children, sweethearts,
brothers sisters, uncles, friends were all left to suffer in silence. The
majority of the mothers died not knowing what had happened to
their sons. Did he perish, or as some of them clung to, had he lost
his memory and was he going to return home some day? No, they
had not lost their memories and they would never return home.

The grieving mothers died never knowing what happened.

Was there a massive government cover-up? Why were the relatives never told the truth? After all, their sons had made the ultimate sacrifice for King and country. The grieving relatives should have been told but they never were. Those who persisted in requesting information from the Admiralty about the loss of their loved ones, were informed it was a wartime secret.

In 1972 the records regarding the sinking of *Dasher* were removed from the secret list and placed in the Public Records Office, Kew. This is not the kind of procedural information that usually becomes known to relatives. Even the families who still persisted in seeking information were never made aware of the existence of these files.

HMS *Dasher* had been built in America as the cargo ship *Rio de Janerio* and hastily converted in Boston into an aircraft carrier for the British, on a lease-lend basis. In effect, the Americans hired an American ship to the British for the duration of hostilities.

When the Americans were advised about the loss of their ship, they laid the blame firmly on 'The British and their lack of safety arrangements regarding stowage of petrol on this type of aircraft carrier.' The Admiralty blamed 'the American safety arrangements, which by British standards were practically non-existent.' Many messages marked Confidential were passed from the Americans to the Admiralty and replies to the American Embassy were classified Secret.

A complete blanket of secrecy shrouded the disaster. Secrecy was imposed on the circumstances surrounding the largest loss of life in home waters next to the *Royal Oak*. But as is usually the case with secrecy, where no hard and fast information is to hand, rumours as to the cause of the disaster started to thrive. Many rumours, theories and opinions survive to this day.

Was the loss of *Dasher* the result of an enemy mine? Or the work of a U-boat torpedo? Was it a case of friendly fire where a stray torpedo from a British submarine in the busy Clyde waters caught the unfortunate *Dasher*? Whispers were heard of an act of sabotage – perhaps a bomb had been planted on board? Perhaps the cause was a mundane one – the ship's engine blown up or an electrical fault in the lighting system? After all, the operational and mechanical record of the *Dasher*, since her recent conversion, had not been good. Several shortcomings had been all too evident in her short life in commission as an aircraft carrier. Alternatively it was suggested a crew member had been smoking during refuelling of aircraft. Some witnesses also encouraged the view that the explosion occurred when a plane crash landed onto the ship.

Whatever the true reason for the catastrophe, the effect on the lives of three hundred and seventy nine of the crew of HMS *Dasher* was terminal. Countless relatives were bereaved for reasons still not clear to this day. Those who witnessed such horrific waste of human life from the island of Arran and from the communities, most notably the town of Ardrossan, on the Ayrshire coast were irredeemably affected by their closeness to disaster.

Of the 379 men who perished, only 23 were accorded an official funeral. Why were so many others buried in secret? Where were they buried and why were no records kept? And why were their bereaved relatives not informed, giving them at least the comfort of knowing finally what had happened?

Fifty nine years on grieving relatives are still seeking answers to their questions. *The Tragedy of HMS Dasher*, published in 1995, provoked a huge number of enquiries from those whose grief, loss and anger has been repressed for fifty years. They want to know more. Many were able to contribute their memories of things said all those years ago. Piece by piece some of the information has helpd to form a picture of what might have happened to bring death to so many young sailors. This book is a response to the demand to know 'What happened to my loved one?' and 'What happened to HMS *Dasher*?' Researches since the last edition also point to one possible reason for the secrecy which was critical in the conduct of World War II and the allied plans to invade mainland Europe.

HMS **Dasher** *sailing in the calm waters of the River Clyde, showing her cargo boat hull and her superimposed timber flight deck*

Silhouetted on her flight deck are the Sea Hurricanes and Swordfish of the Fleet Air Arm

27th March, Disaster Day

09.00 27th March 1943

On leaving Lamlash Bay, Isle of Arran, HMS *Dasher,* **a converted** aircraft carrier with her ship's company of five hundred and twenty eight personnel, sailed in a northerly direction in the Clyde estuary. It was a beautiful calm, sunny day. Captain LAK Boswell DSO, had taken command of the ship two weeks earlier and was well aware that sinkings of merchant ships by the dreaded U-boats had risen from thirty seven ships in January 1943 to sixty three ships in February. In the first ten days of March, forty one ships had been sunk and fifty six sunk in the second ten days, two thirds of which had been lost in convoy. The efforts of his vessel were vital in the war effort. Like her sister ships of the same model, *Dasher* had been detailed to escort duty, to protect the crucial North Atlantic corridor. With the presence of a much valued aircraft carrier in a convoy, the planes could do constant reconnaissance to protect cargo fleets from the attention of the pervasive German U-boats.

Captain Boswell was determined that *Dasher* would have a thorough working-up before her next convoy, to ensure that his ship and crew would be in peak condition.

Number 891 Squadron had just joined *Dasher* and the six Swordfish and six Hurricane aircraft commenced practising take-off and landing exercises. While the aircraft crew practised, *Dasher's* motor launch continually circled the ship. In the event of a plane crash-landing and going over the side into the water, the motor launch would speed towards the plane in an attempt to rescue the stricken pilot. The motor launch was ML528 under the command of Sub Lieutenant ECD Holeman. The crew consisted of Sub Lieutenat RFC Durban, Ordinary Seaman GH Bayliss and Leading Sick Berth Attendant L Bamberger.

After sailing north for approximately five miles, *Dasher* altered course and proceeded south for five miles. Then once again sailed north. This continued all day, with aircraft flying off and touching down on *Dasher's* flight deck.

During the aircraft exercises the ship's crew went about their duties. Captain Boswell was on the bridge with Commander Lane and Sub Lieutenant Helps. Sub Lieutenant John Ferrier from Greenock was standing on the flight deck with two other Sub Lieutenants. The three of them were engine room personnel enjoying the fresh air and admiring the lovely view with the sun highlighting the snow-tipped Arran hills. One of them, Trevor Buxton said, 'When this is all over I will return to this lovely part of the country.' Frank Tetlow agreed and said that he intended to do likewise.

16.30

In the hangar the aircraft were being refuelled. One Hurricane was still on the flight deck waiting to be lowered down into the hangar, where Port Watch and Starboard Watch were making the aircraft secure, under the charge of Petty Officer Reg Dickens. On completion of this duty he instructed the Port Watch to refuel the aircraft and for Starboard Watch to make their way to the mess room, as tea time was approaching. Petty Officer John Mann was also in the hangar standing on a trestle, working on a plane.

The Commanding Officer of 891 Squadron, Lieutenant Commander Nigel Bailey, was in the Squadron office just beneath the flight deck.

Lieutenant Commander Wootton was in the engine room with the duty engine room staff. In the Petty Officers' bathrooms the off-duty Petty Officers were having a wash and shave. All was well aboard *Dasher*, the ship was in the safe waters of the Clyde and the crew, on duty or not, were relaxed.

16.35

Dasher was returning to Lamlash Bay when a message was received from the Commanding Officer at Greenock, instructing Captain Boswell to proceed to the Tail o' the Bank. Outside Lamlash Post Office four local girls were chatting about the ship that was heading for their sheltered bay and happily anticipating the dance that would surely follow that night. The air of excitement felt by the girls was quickly dispelled when they noticed the aircraft carrier changing course and sailing away from the bay in a northerly direction.

Captain Boswell ordered a message to be passed to the Flag Officer at Greenock to lower the boom net which straddled across the Clyde from Dunoon to the Cloch lighthouse. This boom net was to ensure that no enemy submarines could enter the Clyde or the surrounding lochs, to attack the many ships which were sure to be anchored prior to convoy duties. They would have proved an easy target for the U-boat commanders. *Dasher's* estimated time of arrival at the boom net was 1800 hours.

When the message was relayed, Captain Boswell made an announcement over the ship's loudspeakers that leave would be granted to non-duty crew. The result of this message was a happy surge of non-duty men quickly making their way below deck, to the wash rooms. A happy atmosphere prevailed as the men jostled to wash and shave, to be ready to disembark when the ship reached port. Those living within travelling distance of Greenock would be happily heading home that night to make a surprise visit to their loved ones.

Throughout the ship, some crew were carrying out their duties. Eighteen year old fireman Peter Leach, from Burton-on-Trent, who had joined the ship only three days previously, was on the flight deck, familiarizing himself with the fire fighting apparatus. Also on the flight deck were a number of Fleet Air Arm personnel who had been involved in the safe departure and arrival of the aircraft during the all-day exercise.

The crew noted that sailing in the vicinity were HMS *Isle of Sark*, a radar training ship, which was four miles south, and the French corvette *La Capricieuse*, which was five miles north. Within one mile of them were two small coasters, the SS *Cragsman* and the SS *Lithium*.

Sub Lieutenant John Ferrier had completed washing and shaving. As a Greenock man, he would be going ashore on leave. John was talking to one of his friends, Bob Wanless in Bob's cabin. John was telling his latest joke.

The atmosphere on board the ship was one of relaxation. After all the ship was in a 'safe area', at a position six miles from Ardrossan harbour (renamed HMS *Fortitude* by the Admiralty). HMS *Fortitude* was home to the biggest mine-sweeping fleet in Scotland. Within ten miles of the ship lay the Isle of Bute and the Cumbrae islands. Cumbrae had a purpose-built U-boat detecting station. The purpose of the building was an open secret and the locals referred to it as 'Hush-Hush'.

As for the Isle of Bute, the authorities had commandeered a bungalow and transformed it into a 'listening post' to enable them to detect any German submarine, should a U-boat Kapitan be so brave as to try and enter the Clyde. Well may *Dasher's* crew relax.

But at 4.39pm the clock was ticking away and in sixty seconds time, a momentous event would take place that would have a life shattering and drastic effect on everyone on board.

16.40

Suddenly the ship shuddered violently as a horrendous explosion took place. On the bridge the officer of the watch shouted, 'Look at that.' Captain Boswell and the officers on the bridge looked in astonishment at the ship's aircraft lift soaring, perfectly vertical, high into the air. Standing on the lift were a handful of the Fleet Air Arm crew. The aircraft lift, weighing in excess of two tons, continued rising until it reached a height of approximately sixty feet before plunging into the sea, portside, narrowly missing *Dasher*. The four men who had been innocently standing on the lift, prior to the explosion, were lost, with no hope of rescue.

John Mann, who had been working in the hangar was blown off

the trestle he had been standing on and knocked breathless. Worse was to befall the Fleet Air Arm crew who had just been dismissed and were in their mess deck enjoying supper. All were lost instantly.

Smoke and flames were rising from the aircraft lift shaft and the flight deck was buckled up to half the length of the hangar. To starboard holes had burst open in the ship's side, out of which smoke and flames were belching. Almost immediately after the explosion every machine on *Dasher* stopped. The lights went out and there were no ship's noises.

The vessel started to settle by the stern. However the buoyancy in the hangar was resisting the pull at the stern. The aircraft carrier started to groan and creak, metal plates sprung from their welded positions as the bow and stern fought a battle. To the men on the ship, the noises were frightening.

Twenty seconds after the lights went out, the emergency generator was activated and the lights in some parts of the ship came back on, giving the crew below deck false hope. But they went back out almost immediately. There was no power and below deck the ship was in complete darkness.

On the bridge, Captain Boswell ordered Lt Commander Lane to find out what was happening. As the Lt Commander made his way below deck, more and more fires were starting. The grinding noises of a dying ship could be heard as he encountered smoke, flames and an onrush of water on deck three. As he retraced his steps, back to the bridge, he quickly checked the cabins and offices to ensure that they were empty.

As *Dasher* commenced to settle by the stern, with her bows slowly rising out of the water, the damage control teams reported to Captain Boswell that a violent fire was taking place in the after-end of the hangar, the Fleet Air Arm mess deck was completely destroyed, there was a serious fire in the engine room, there was no power in any part of *Dasher* and there was rapid flooding and many fires throughout the ship. Commander Boswell immediately gave the order, 'ABANDON SHIP, ABANDON SHIP'. These words were relayed to all parts of the aircraft carrier and every man on board made his way as best as he could to safety.

With the ship in complete darkness below decks, the crew members who had joined the vessel in America were the ones who knew their way to the corridors, the gangways, the ladders, and to the hangar. From there the crew had a chance of escape by jumping between sixty and ninety feet into the cold waters of the Clyde.

In the engine room, Commander Wootton instructed his men to abandon ship and they quickly tried to reach the hangar. As the crew were running along dark corridors or trying to climb ladders, they were encountering other shipmates going in the opposite direction. On telling them that they were going the wrong way, the reply they received was that the men were making for their lockers to retrieve their precious possessions, before jumping off the ship. Tragically they were never to be seen again.

Below deck, the crew were hampered badly, not only by the darkness, but also by the ladders, as only one man at a time could climb up. As they waited their turn to climb or make their way slowly along the dark passageways, the men could hear the groans of the dying ship.

The incoming water was hitting against hot pipes, steam was hissing and doors were buckling as Petty Officer Jack Verlaque, from Paisley, guided a group of young lads to safety. Jack had joined *Dasher* in the United States and was familiar with the layout of the ship. Shouting words of encouragement, he led them to ladders leading to the hangar. As they followed him up, there was an air of relief in the group. However when Jack stepped off the ladder into the hangar he was met with a bombardment of bullets from the aircrafts' ammunition. The bullets were exploding due to the intense heat from the many fires in the hangar. Jack shouted to the men to get back down and this led to confusion as they were so near to a jumping off point.

All the time, *Dasher* was slowly pointing her bows to the sky, rising out of the water. Meantime, Jack led his young shipmates another way up to the hangar. As they were making their way to safety, they could hear the cries of men shouting for firemen and for first aid help.

Petty Officer John Stamp from South Shields was in a position to jump overboard when he heard cries for help coming from behind a jammed watertight door. The cries for help were from doomed young men. The Petty Officer made the brave decision to remain on board to open the door. Being of strong build, he forced the door open to find around twenty young ratings trapped in the dark passageway. As the ratings quickly made their escape out of the dark corridor and jumped overboard, the door was being forced closed by the onrush of water.

At this point John Stamp could have saved his own life by jumping overboard. However in the highest tradition of the Royal Navy, he remained where he was, with one foot holding the heavy watertight door open and his back braced against the bulkhead until all the ratings had escaped. By now it was too late for John to save himself. He paid the ultimate price by remaining on board to save so many young lives.

Below deck, Petty Officer Jeffrey Gray had just placed his overall suit into a bucket to soak. He was walking towards the Master-at-Arms office, to post a letter to his wife when the explosion occurred and all the lights went out. By the light of the flames from the hangar lighting up the passageway, he was able to make his way up the port ladder into the hangar and out through the forward door where a number of sailors were. Although he was in his underwear, they recognised him as a Petty Officer and obeyed his order to 'release all Carley rafts'. On jumping into the water, he swam to the raft which was furthest away, thereby giving those who were not strong swimmers the chance to board the Carley rafts nearest the ship.

In the wheelhouse, after twenty to thirty seconds, the deafening ringing of the alarm bell ceased. Enclosed in the wheelhouse, Tom Dawson and Danny McCarthy were left in eerie silence, oblivious to the drama unfolding throughout the ship. With communication completely broken down and being unable to contact the bridge, it was the tilting of the deck that convinced them that they should evacuate. Both Tom and Danny stepped onto the open deck and quickly jumped overboard. Once in the water, Tom Dawson swam fifty feet clear of the ship and then turned to watch her dying moments. He saw the one remaining aircraft on the flight deck break clear of its lashings and slither over the side.

On the flight deck, the Commanding Officer of 891 Squadron, Lt Commander Nigel Bailey was about to jump off *Dasher* when he heard a cry of 'look out!' He turned just in time to see one of his own Sea Hurricanes careering down the flight deck haphazardly towards him. The aircraft was completely out of control and the Squadron Leader had to take evasive action by running clear of the plane and watched as it unceremoniously slid off the ship. On landing in the water, the aircraft immediately disappeared under the waves.

The eighteen year old fireman, Tom Leach, had been knocked unconscious by the blast and was lying on the flight deck. Two of the crew grabbed the unconscious fireman and jumped from a height of eighty feet into the water, each of them holding onto him. On surfacing, the two crewmen swam for their lives away from *Dasher* and like the majority of those in the water, they turned to watch the bow of their aircraft carrier point straight to the sky as she slowly slipped out of sight. Even at this final stage in the death of the ship, some of the crew were still jumping off *Dasher* as she went down. For others, it was too late. They were below deck, unable to reach safety.

Also below deck, kitchen equipment, lockers and every other object that was not secure was being hurled around. In all the mess decks, plates, utensils, tables and chairs were being smashed to pieces. The doors to crews' lockers were springing open and the personal contents were spilling out into the maelstrom.

Just prior to the explosion, Air Mechanic William Macdonald had opened his locker and removed his kitbag, as he was intending to have a wash and shave. He slung his kitbag under his arm in order to remove his shaving gear. The tremendous force of the explosion knocked him unconscious and thrust him through a hole which had suddenly appeared in the side of the ship.

At the same time, the crew of *Dasher's* Motor Launch, ML528, who were staring in disbelief at the terrible eruption from their ship, heard the command from Sub Lieutenant Holeman, 'Full Speed Ahead.'

One of those on board Motor Launch *528* was Leading Sick Berth Attendant Lionel E Banberger, who relates the story.

'We had been circulating our ship in the event of an aircraft over-shooting and landing in the water. I was in the wheelhouse at the time and I saw the aircraft lift rising high into the sky. I then saw my shipmates jumping overboard.

'As we moved in to carry out a rescue we picked up a seaman who was clutching his kitbag. He was about four hundred yards from *Dasher* and he was practically un-conscious. I asked him how he managed to get in the water so far away from the ship. He replied that he was blown out.

'I put the seaman into the sick bay and asked him his name. He replied, William Macdonald. I made my way forward back on deck and saw *Dasher* going under.

'We picked up another seventeen shipmates out of the water and twenty two out of Carley rafts. William Mac-Donald's face, hands and chest were burned and the skin in his hands had been blown off. He spoke coherently and there was no misunderstanding about what he was saying as he had a good hold of himself.'

CHAPTER 2

SHIP REPORTED SINKING

Ardrossan's North Shore was a popular walk for the locals and many were taking advantage of the fine spring afternoon. No one paid particular attention to the many ships in this busy stretch of water between the Ayrshire coast and the Isle of Arran. The Firth of Clyde was known to them as a well-protected safe haven for shipping.

When the explosion was heard the strollers paused and looked westward, out to sea. A huge thick pall of black smoke was seen to rise from a large ship. As the locals watched, a voice was heard to say, 'An exercise – they have to practise, I suppose.'

Slowly the strollers moved on. After all, it was perfectly reasonable that in the present wartime conditions a naval vessel would be involved in firing practice and putting up a smoke screen. Tea-time was approaching and the naval exercise was of little interest to them. They were completely unaware of the life and death drama taking place, involving five hundred and twenty eight young men from all parts of the United Kingdom.

At HMS *Fortitude*, (Ardrossan Harbour), a Royal Navy priority signal was received stating, 'ALL VESSELS PUT TO SEA IMMEDIATELY. MAJOR RESCUE OPERATION INVOLVING ROYAL NAVY AIRCRAFT CARRIER HMS *Dasher*. SHIP REPORTED SINKING.'

On receipt of the message, all ships within the harbour cast off *(above and previous page) These pictures taken by a seaman aboard the radar training ship HMS* Isle of Sark *show the* Isle of Sark *racing towards the scene of the explosion.*

The Isle of Sark *picked up oil-covered survivors as shown (above), thirty five were hauled out of the water by this one ship alone, three of whom died of their injuries on board.*

The crews of all ships, navy and civilian, involved in the rescue operation were ordered not to speak about the incident

and made their way to the assistance of *Dasher*. One of the departing vessels was minesweeper, MS23. Even though two thirds of the crew were ashore on leave, the commanding officer had no hesitation in joining the rescue.

In the Royal Navy Sick Bay, at 8 South Crescent, Ardrossan, the medical staff were preparing for a large number of casualties.

The local cinemas were busy as usual on a Saturday. The people had a choice of viewing. The Regal was showing Charlie Chaplin's *Gold Rush* while the La Scala screened a propaganda documentary *Coastal Command*. The third cinema in Saltcoats, The Countess was featuring *Bad Man of Wyoming*. However all performances were interrupted by a message flashed onto the screen ordering, 'ALL FIRST AID AND CIVIL DEFENCE PERSONNEL REPORT TO THEIR POSTS IMMEDIATELY.'

As the rescue operation swung into action and the ships closed in on the disaster area, *Dasher's* survivors could be seen in the water. Considering the circumstances, morale was high as the survivors could see the armada of vessels closing in at speed. Two different groups in the water started singing as men held onto those who had been injured. Peter Leach, the fireman who had been hauled off the ship, was floating, still unconscious, whilst being supported by a Royal Air Force Sergeant

Their ship was gone, the water was cold and although help was coming, it could not come quickly enough for the survivors, who were by now mostly huddled in groups. As they swam or held on to floats, they could smell aviation fuel and diesel. *Dasher's* 75,000 gallons of fuel for her engines and 20,000 gallons of aviation fuel for her aircraft were surging from the burst tanks. The men were black with the thick slimy fuels. Friends joked with friends, 'You look like a black man.' 'So do you,' was the reply.

They could see the armada of rescue ships fast approaching, sailing from north, south, east and west. No matter in which direction the survivors looked, ships were coming. It was just a matter of time before they would be enjoying the warmth of an engine room and drinking a glass of rum or whisky, or so they thought.

Commander Lane was swimming from Carley raft to Carley raft and from group to group, shouting words of encouragement. 'Don't worry lads, it won't be long now.'

Unfortunately fate was to play another cruel blow. As the rescue ships came closer and closer there was a sudden whoosing noise. The aviation fuel and diesel ignited. Flames and searing heat swept through the survivors. Men swam as quickly as they could in a race for their lives. They swam away from the fast-moving deadly flames which were rapidly covering the surface of the sea. Others, in desperation, took a deep breath and dived under the water in a bid to escape certain death amid the burning inferno. Those that resurfaced too quickly perished. Never was the saying, 'You are not a survivor until you are out of the water', more true than now. Young men who had survived the sinking of their ship, lost their lives to the deadly flames. What was left was the thick black choking smoke, the overpowering smell of oil and diesel, coupled with flames fanning in the distance. Intermingled with this were the shouted commands and the screams of those injured and badly burned.

Some of the survivors remained on Carley rafts. The lucky ones, the flames missed; for others the flames were headed straight towards them. Those who saw the flames heading in their direction used their hands and feet to propel the rafts away from the deadly danger. Many perished in the flames. Leslie Falla was one of them. Leslie was a non swimmer and after jumping from *Dasher* he had been helped onto a Carley raft. The heat was so intense that his shipmates could render no assistance to him when he was engulfed in flames. His dying screams could be heard by those who could not help, due the intense heat.

Within minutes, the survivors who had been suffering in the cold waters of the Clyde, were decimated by the heat of burning fuel from their own ship. Life was too cruel.

On seeing the height of the flames and the speed at which they were travelling, the officer in command of the rescue operation ordered all ships to 'KEEP CLEAR, WE CANNOT AFFORD TO LOSE ANOTHER SHIP THIS DAY.'

On receipt of the message, all Royal Navy rescue ships including *Dasher's* own Motor Launch 528 kept well clear of the rescue area. As the thick black smoke rose higher into the air, the ships that were keeping clear commenced lowering their lifeboats. These lifeboats then had to be rowed by eight men to the disaster site. This was taking up much valuable time as those who had been burned were now suffering from the coldness of the Clyde. The men who had evaded the flames were now suffering from the cold waters and a numbness was setting in.

The officers on board the Royal Navy ships, who had been ordered to keep their vessels clear of the burning sea, were astonished to watch the SS *Cragsman*, a small coastal vessel, sail directly towards the burning inferno. The chugging noise of the single diesel engine could be heard loud and clear as the *Cragsman* sailed straight into the smoke and flames and disappeared completely from view. It was feared that another ship was lost.

Captain James Templeton of the *Cragsman*, the ship's mate and another crew member were from Northern Ireland, seven were from the Hebrides, two from Paisley, one from Dalry in Ayrshire and one from Glasgow. The crew of the vessel, which was on passage from Stornoway to Glasgow, watched in horror as hundreds of men struggled for survival in the water, amidst the terrible flames. The tremendous heat, the cold choppy waves and strong current took their toll as the *Cragsman* crew leaned overboard to grasp the slippery hands of those in the water. As it was too dangerous for the vessel to stop in the burning water, it chugged slowly onwards.

It was a nightmare situation for all concerned. The struggling survivors tried to swim close to the rescue vessel to reach the out-stretched hands of their would-be rescuers. Many of them just could not swim fast enough as the *Cragsman* slowly sailed through the catastrophic scene. Others managed to grasp the out-stretched hands of those on board. However when the hands clasped with a firm life-saving grip, the by now, fast flowing current split the slippy oily hands cruelly apart. The *Cragsman* crew could only watch in dire dismay as the men they had within their grasp, the grasp of safety, slipped from them and the *Dasher* men drifted further and further away, screaming for help.

The *Cragsman* had by now played its part in this terrible drama which was completely unseen by the officers on the Royal Navy ships. Captain Templeton was well aware that his vessel was in great danger and that they could do no more. It was heart-wrenching for all as the vessel made its way from the scene of carnage.

The chugging noise of the single diesel engine was heard again as the *Cragsman* slowly reappeared from the thick black smoke and flames with fourteen survivors – one survivor for each member of the crew.

As Captain Templeton navigated from the fiery inferno, the small coastal vessel SS *Lithium* was bravely heading straight into the flames and smoke, there to repeat the heroism of the *Cragsman*

Captain JF Terreta of the *Lithium* did not hesitate in moving his vessel close to the survivors. Once more the survivors saw a chance of saving their lives and made a frantic bid to swim towards the would-be rescuers. The stronger ones amongst them were able to fight against the strong current which swept the weaker ones away. The crew of the *Lithium* were desperately reaching out, shouting words of encouragement, as they hauled as many on board as was humanly possible. Some were torn from their grasp as, like the *Cragsman* crew, their oil-covered hands couldn't keep a hold and the poor souls slipped away.

The *Lithium* crew, like the crew of the *Cragsman* were devastated to have had so many within their grasp and then witness them being swept away. Every time this happened, the rescuers threw overboard anything that would float, anything that could possibly offer another chance for those in he water.

As the first of the *Dasher* men were hauled on board the *Lithium* they were ushered quickly down to the heat of the engine room by the crew which comprised the captain, three engineers, Ernie the stoker, Jack Wrench from Wales who was the ship's gunner and Stan McKenzie from Aberdeen.

As firm grips parted and the unfortunate slipped from safety, their shouts for help as they drifted away were to remain with the brave *Lithium* crew. Remain with them and haunt them for the rest of their lives.

As more and more were saved, the engine room quickly filled up and the rescued stood on the deck of the small three hundred ton vessel which was already fully loaded with sulphur. They huddled shoulder to shoulder until no more could be brought on board. The ship was now lying so low in the water, if any more had been brought on board, the vessel would have been in great danger of sinking.

The men in the water watched the *Lithium* cease the rescue operation. No more could be helped on board as the coaster sailed on, packed to overflowing. Stan McKenzie from Aberdeen relates,

'Very soon we had so many on board, we were taking in water as we were up to the gunnels. We were leaving so many behind, it was heartbreaking. As there was a strong current flowing, it was sweeping those poor souls past us. As they were being swept past, they were screaming for help. We threw overboard ladders, ropes, mops, brushes, anything that would float and possibly help those we were reluctantly leaving in the water. We threw overboard anything that they could hold onto until more help arrived. One of the survivors I helped on board said that he was an engineer from the engine room. Unfortunately he died on board our vessel.'

As the *Lithium* slowly departed, having to leave so many behind, as if on cue, the first of the Royal Navy lifeboats arrived, each with eight men straining at the oars. They came from the French vessel *La Capricieuse*, the radar training ship *Isle of Sark*, the Knight class armed trawler *Sir Galahad*, HMS *Attacker* and the Ardrossan-based minesweepers.

As the flames subsided, the Royal Navy ships, as one, quickly sailed in to the rescue. The *Isle of Sark* picked up thirty five, three of whom died on board. Of the twenty six the *La Capricieuse* picked up, seven died on board.

Peter Taylor from Spalding, Linconshire takes up the story.

'We were engaged in an exercise with unarmed British submarines. By unarmed, I mean they were not carrying torpedoes. On hearing the dreadful explosion the captain cancelled the exercise and headed towards *Dasher* at full speed. Although we were conscious that the sinking may have been the result of enemy action, *La Capricieuse* did not deviate but went straight to the scene where we saw men and debris in the water.

'The captain positioned our ship as close to the flames as possible and had our boats lowered to pick up survivors. I watched the rescue operation from the bridge and could see survivors being pulled from the water with all possible haste. Even when it required members of the boat crews having to jump into the water to assist.

'I had not seen drowned men in the sea before and had not realised that they floated upright so that the crown of their head was level with the surface. It was while searching for them I saw a sailor appear on the port side. He was upright in the water and his head was bobbing about the surface as though he was still alive and trying to take air. The Officer on Watch gave me permission to dive in and go to him.

'I got him back to our ship and he was taken on board but he was dead. I was thickly covered with oil – all my clothing was saturated and spoiled. We were all in a similar state. In fact it was difficult to distinguish between ship's company and survivors. There were no onlookers. Every available member of our ship's company was involved voluntarily and showed great concern to the survivors. Everything we had was made available to them and every effort was made to revive and resuscitate others.

'I do not think any more could have been done by any man. Every available space on board was taken up with bodies, even our cabins. When it became apparent that we could do no more we sailed from the scene. We had injured survivors requiring medical attention and there were by then many other ships searching and rescuing. No one gave up looking until forced to do so. There were many acts of bravery that day. We sailed to Ardrossan where survivors were taken ashore, after which, we proceeded to our base at the Holy Loch. I do remember being told enroute to the Holy Loch that the sinking of HMS *Dasher* was due to a plane crash-landing on the flight deck.'

Alex White, an Able Seaman from South Shields on board the *Isle of Sark*, was ordered to join a lifeboat party and row to the assistance of those in the water. Alex relates,

'I was a member of the lifeboat crew that took part in the rescue of survivors and bodies. It was evident that some were floating face down with their heads and feet in the water but the remainder of their bodies were above the water. This was because their lifejackets were tied around their middle. This was common practice, when in fact, the lifejacket should have been tied close to their chests.'

As darkness fell, the *Lithium* transferred the sixty men she had saved, to the *Sir Galahad*. The *Cragsman* also transferred those they had plucked from the water. Of the fourteen they saved, three sadly had died on board. As darkness fell the rescue operation was called off and as there was nothing else they could do to assist, the *Lithium* and *Cragsman* proceeded on their journeys.

All Royal Navy ships were ordered to proceed to Ardrossan, with the exception of the *Isle of Sark* being instructed to report to Greenock.

From the time of the explosion to the complete disappearance of *Dasher*, only eight minutes had elapsed. Not long enough time to allow all on board to evacuate the ship. Remarkably most of those in the engine room made it to safety. As the men in the water watched, their ship slipped beneath the waves, taking with her many young men who were not ready to die.

The aircraft carrier came to rest upright on the sea bed with her bow pointing towards Arran. When it became impossible to render further assistance, due to darkness falling and the dearth of cries of help, the heartbreaking rescue operation reluctantly came to an end. Signals were passed to all Royal Navy rescue ships in the vicinity,

'THIS INCIDENT IS NOT, REPEAT, NOT TO BE SPOKEN ABOUT'

When the survivors were helped ashore, they were also ordered not to talk about the disaster.

Survivors and casualties were brought ashore at Ardrossan and at Greenock. These photos were taken at Greenock and show the injured and deceased being taken from HMS Isle of Sark

CHAPTER 3

SURVIVORS IN ARDROSSAN

On that bleak dark Saturday night, as the returning ships entered Ardrossan harbour, there was very little for the beleaguered survivors to see. The first ambulance to arrive at the harbour was driven by a member of the Sick Bay staff, Harry Judd. He watched as the rescue flotilla arrived. *La Capricieuse* was the first to berth, followed by the motor launch ML528 and then the first of the home-based minesweepers.

Due to the wartime restrictions, the town was in complete darkness. The *Dasher* survivors slowly shuffled down the gangways wrapped in blankets, most with bare feet and little protection from the cold. On reaching the harbour-side they were quickly helped into the waiting ambulances or ambulance trailers. The wounded were assisted by the medical personnel. The deceased were shrouded in the Union Jack, placed on a stretcher and carried off the ships. As a mark of respect, all medical staff had 'Caps Off'.

When Harry Judd's ambulance was packed with badly burned sailors, he drove to the nearby local Sick Bay. On the way, it passed the ever growing fleet of first aid vehicles with doctors, nurses and stretcher bearers. Every available emergency vehicle and staff from the surrounding area had been dispatched to the harbour to help cope with the expected large number of casualties. In addition to the conventional ambulances, there were numerous ambulance trailers. These consisted of a metal chassis mounted on two car wheels and were capable of carrying up to six stretcher cases. The sides consisted of waterproof canvas which could be rolled up and tied in position. This allowed access for the casualties to be secured two abreast, three tiers high.

A gruesome sight was witnessed by many as one of the ambulance trailers turned a corner. A limp arm appeared from under the canvas and dangled over the side of the trailer with the hand trailing along the ground. The driver of the speeding vehicle was completely unaware of the most unfortunate circumstances of one of the *Dasher* casualties in his charge.

The casualties must have suffered terribly while being transported in the trailers which were towed by cars to the emergency centres. The ambulances took the casualties to one of four destinations: the Royal Navy Sick Bay at 8 South Crescent, Ardrossan; the First Aid Post in Saltcoats; Ballochmyle Hospital, thirty miles south of Ardrossan; and the morgue at Ardrossan's Harbour Street.

Those not requiring medical attention were taken to the Royal Navy base in Glasgow Street. The officers were taken to the Eglinton Hotel in Ardrossan's Princes Street and the ratings were billeted with the locals of Ardrossan. Every survivor was ordered not to talk about the disaster or the loss of their ship.

On that fateful day which the residents of Ardrossan will never forget, the first signal to HMS *Fortitude* had stated, 'PREPARE FOR A LARGE NUMBER OF CASUALTIES.'

The large number expected was reflected by the huge fleet of approximately fifty ambulances and ambulance trailers that arrived at the harbour. Many of them returned to their base that night as they were classed as Not Required. Out of *Dasher's* crew of 528, the large number of casualties expected was unfortunately greatly diminished due to the dreadful number of fatalities, caused in part by the sea igniting.

During the next few days, as the survivors strolled through the town, they would pass the time of day with the locals but not once did they mention any details of their ship, the disaster, or what they had suffered. They were obeying orders not to talk about the tragedy. They were also instructed not to leave the town of Ardrossan until further notice.

Sub Lieutenant John Ferrier from the nearby town of Greenock, was well aware that the disaster could have been witnessed by the locals of the Ayrshire and Arran coast. He was also aware that news of the tragedy would spread like wildfire. As he was concerned about what news would reach his family and his fiancée, John travelled home by bus, in order to correct any unfounded stories that would soon be in circulation.

John's concern proved to be well-founded as the loss of the aircraft carrier had been witnessed by many on the Ayrshire and Arran coastlines. The name *Dasher* was being linked to the terrible disaster by Royal Navy personnel stationed at Greenock.

As news of the sea tragedy and rescue operation began spreading by word of mouth, a telephone call was made to the *Daily Record*, one of Scotland national newspapers, reporting the sea tragedy. The following day, Sunday 28th March, the young newspaper telephonist who received the call, visited her cousin, Donald McCall, a fourteen year old shipping enthusiast from Glasgow. She was aware of Donald's keen interest in shipping matters and during her visit, she said to him in hushed tones, 'Yesterday an aircraft carrier blew up and sank in the Clyde, between Ardrossan and Arran.'

Mrs Mary Murchie, a resident of Ardrossan and wife of the chief officer aboard the coaster, *Lady Dorothy*, had friends visiting her that fateful afternoon. They were naval officer Alex Stonebridge and his wife, Ruth. The three of them were sitting watching the ships in the Clyde and admiring the lovely view when there was a huge bang which shook every window in the house. The two women were quite frightened as they saw the flames and black smoke. The Royal Navy officer immediately jumped out of his chair, grabbed his gas mask and told the two women to remain in the house. As he ran out to report for duty, Mrs Murchie and her friend thought that it was an air raid.

From a front room window they watched the large number of

ambulances speeding to and from the harbour. Mrs Murchie remembers, 'Word went round the town that a large ship had sunk just off the shore.'

Over the weekend the gruesome task of removing oil and cleaning the bodies of the deceased was carried out by the local undertaker, assisted by a police sergeant. Lt Commander Lane was in charge of identification of bodies. On completion of this very sad task, the dreaded telegrams were dispatched on Monday 29th March. They were received the same day by the unsuspecting families. They read,

DEEPLY REGRET TO REPORT DEATH OF_____.
FUNERAL ARRANGEMENTS WILL BE COMMUNICATED DIRECT TO YOU FROM FLAG OFFICER IN CHARGE, GREENOCK

The telegrams containing the navy funeral arrangements arrived the same day. They read,

FUNERAL WILL TAKE PLACE FROM NAVAL BASE ARDROSSAN AT 1400 ON WEDNESDAY 31ST MARCH

A list of those admitted to Ballochmyle Hospital in the twenty four hours to 28th March 1943 revealed that twenty members of *Dasher*'s crew were receiving medical attention.

William Balfour Addison (43)
Petty Officer FAA
RYRB/14494

Ronald Hague (21)
AB Seaman RDF
P/JX271957

Barry James Barnett (21)
1st Class Air Mechanic FAA 816
Sqdn. FX/80707

Arthur Hughes (25)
AB Seaman LFD
CJX/155789

Frederick Thomas Cole (38)
Asst Steward
NAP/107711

Robert Jenkins (31)
O/TELS
CJX/250524

Neil Cameron Murray (23)
Steward
NAP/R 158176

Eric Richard Hall (20)
Leading Airman FAA 816 Sqdn.
FX/89076

John Lenard Philips (25)
Storekeeper
NAP/R 203519

Gerard Heeney (32)
Steward
APR/35483

Edward Rhodes (22)
AB Seaman
CJX/258532

William McPherson (32)
Leading Stoker
NAP/R 230432

Thomas William Townsend (24)
AB Seaman
C/OSX 19786

Alfred Norman Penman (22)
AB Seaman (HMS *Pembroke*)
CJX/178003

Robert Watts (21)
AB Seaman
CJX/158015

Cledwyn Robinson (23)
AB Seaman
CJX/168614

William George Caley (27)
Leading Seaman
CSSX 26817

Edward Cyril Traill (31)
Petty Officer (HMS *Mersey*)
T/124X

Raymond Coles (20)
AB Seaman
JX/301801

William Albert Wall (32)
L Writer 891 Sqdn. DN FAA
P/DX18

Officers Killed, Brought Ashore
Buxton, Trevor Victor   Ty Act Sub Lt (E) RNVR
Haughie, William Pratt   Ty Act Sub Lt (E) RNVR
McFarlane, J   Ty Sub Lt
Price, Fleetwood Elwin   Lieutenant
Stallard-Penoyre, Ralph Carnac Baker Lt RN
Walker, John Russell   Sub Lt

Ratings Killed, Brought Ashore

Costar, Ernest C	Able Seaman C/JX.190282	
Craig, Archibald B	Leading Seaman	RDF P/JX.212188
Crawford, James	Diesel Greaser T.124.X	
Davis, Cecil J	Ordinary Telegraphist	C/JX.271890
Gillies, William	Leading Writer Temporary D/SR.16610	
Harper, Harry	Able Seaman C/JX.260671	
Kane, James	Able Seaman C/SSX.18806	
Lawrence, Arthur C	Diesel Greaser T124.X	
Liddle, Richard	Ordinary Seaman C/JX.374403	
Martin, Thomas	Able Seaman C/JX.168035	
Melville, John	Ordinary Coder	C/JX.361352
Neath, Ronald	Leading Radio Mechanic P/MX.100601	
Percival, George HM	Ordinary Seaman C/JX.359516	
Woolaghan, Sylvester	Able Seaman C/JX.212950	
Wright, Jack S	Able Seaman C/J.110766	

Having identified the survivors, the deceased and those admitted to hospital, the remainder of the crew were classified as missing. The ship's list of those on board was checked and rechecked, before over three hundred and fifty telegrams were dispatched to the loved ones, reporting them missing.

The final list read:

Survivors – 149; Deceased brought ashore and identified – 23 .

The proportion of the crew dead and missing was 72%.

The loss was:

Royal Navy	346
Merchant Navy	27
Royal Air Force	3
N.A.F.F.I	3
Total loss	379

CHAPTER 4
FUNERAL SERVICES

Although the Royal Navy made every effort possible to identify
the dead, this was a dreadful and impossible task due to the nature
of the disaster. Twelve of the identified deceased brought ashore at
Ardrossan were accorded full naval honours in the town. The
coffins, each draped in the Union Jack, rested on an open-backed
lorry. There were two highly polished lorries, each carrying six
coffins.

Immediately behind, were the relatives of the deceased, in cars
provided by the Royal Navy. The cars were followed by the firing
party and then a naval band. A large representation of the Royal
Navy and the Woman's Royal Naval Services brought up the rear.

As a mark of respect the shops along the funeral route in
Ardrossan remained closed. Many people lined the main street and
watched in silence. The local school children were brought out to
the front of their school to stand as the funeral procession passed
by. One lady was heard to whisper, 'It's like a royal funeral.'

The cortege, under the command of Captain J L Fields, proceeded
slowly towards Ardrossan Cemetery. The drums were muffled as
the band played the Death March. It was a very emotional occasion,
carried out with great dignity by all the immaculately turned out
Royal Navy personnel.

The procession solemnly made its way to the rear of the walled cemetery where the young sailors were to be laid to rest. As each coffin was lowered into the cold ground a volley of shots was fired overhead. At the end of the ceremony and funeral service the command was given to the naval band, Quick March. They quickly marched from the cemetery whilst playing the tune *Colonel Bogey*. The drums were no longer muffled.

The twelve young men laid to rest in Mid West Section B of Ardrossan Cemetery, were:

> Lieutenant RCB Stallard-Penoyre (age 29);
> Flight Sergeant A Grieve (age 28);
> Sub-Lieutenant Trevor Victor Buxton (age 25);
> Sub-Lieutenant William P Haughie (age 25);
> Able Seaman Ernest C Costar (age 23);
> Able Seaman Jack S Wright (age 34);
> Able Seaman James Kane;
> Able Seaman Thomas J Martin (age 24);
> Arthur C Lawrence, Greaser;
> Cecil J Davis, Telegraphist (age 21);
> John Melville, Coder (age 37);
> James Crawford, Fireman & Greaser.

Four bereaved families arranged with the Royal Navy for their loved ones to be taken to their home town for private burial. They were:

> Leading Seaman Archibald B Craig, Buried Paisley;
> Sub Lieutenant John Russel Walker,
> > Buried Newton Mearns, Glasgow;
> Able Seaman Sylvester Woolaghan,
> > Buried Frizington, Cumbria;
> Sub Lieutenant John Lyle McFarlane, Buried Greenock.

The Royal Navy held a funeral service in Greenock Cemetery, where six of John L McFarlane's shipmates were buried with full military honours. They were:

> William Gillies, Leading Writer;
> Able Seaman Harry Harper;

Ordinary Seaman Richard Liddle;
Ronald Neath, Leading Radio Mechanic;
Ordinary Seaman George HM Percival;
Lieutenant Fleetwood E Price, Gunnery Officer.

A number of deceased were unidentified for two reasons:
1. It was impossible for the Officer in Charge of Indentification of Bodies to know the names and to recognise all 527 crew on board *Dasher*.
2. Some of the deceased were unrecognizable due to burns.
For the unidentified, there was to be no public Royal Navy funeral.

The survivors assumed that their close friends and shipmates had been brought ashore at other ports. They were never informed of the number of casualties or the number of those missing. When they went home on survivors' leave, they thought that some day, somewhere, they would meet up with their friends from *Dasher*. It was not to be.

One other funeral service was for William Macdonald, an Air Mechanic with the Fleet Air Arm. William was the unfortunate crewman who had been blown four hundred yards, through a hole in the side of his ship and picked out of the water by Motor Launch *528*. On arrival at HMS *Fortitude* William was taken to the local Sick Bay. As he was so badly burned, it was deemed wise not to move him to Ballochmyle Hospital. Although William received the best of treatment from the doctors and medical staff, he passed away thirteen days after the catastrophe. His parents were at their son's bedside. They had travelled from the north of Scotland to be with him. William was buried beside his shipmates in Ardrossan Cemetery, with full Naval honours.

GV Rudolph from Harlow in Essex, relates,

'I was based in Ardrossan and served on board minesweepers. I was in the seaman's mission when a phone call came through ordering navy personnel to Report Back. On reaching the harbour, all minesweepers had sailed to take part in the rescue operation. One week later, I attended the funeral of the men whose bodies had been washed up on the beach.'

During the period of the bodies being washed up at North Shore, Ardrossan, it is documented and remembered that the area was closed to the public and was patrolled by Royal Navy personnel. Closer to the town, a gentleman found a pair of high powered binoculars on the beach. On examination, they were found to be of naval origin and were returned to the appropriate authorities. For many weeks, the beach was littered with fruit, debris, oil, sailors' hats and uniforms. The beach was badly contaminated by black diesel oil and still shows signs of contamination to this day.

CHAPTER 5

MISSING ON ACTIVE SERVICE

Officer casualties

Allan, William Lothian	Ty Act Lt Cdr (E) RNR
Banister, Maurice James	Ty Sub Lt (A) RNVR
Barker, Frank Ernest Joseph	Ty Sub-Lt (E) RNVR
Cameron, Angus	Ty Act Sub-Lt (E) RNVR
Cuthbert, John Nicholas	Schoolmaster RN
Davies, Kenneth William	Lieutenant RNR
Havers, Patrick Howard	Lt Cdr RN
Hughes, John	Ty Lt RN
Hutchinson, Robert	Ty Act Sub-Lt (E), RNVR
Johnston, Owen Temple	Sub-Lt RN
Langley, John Robert	Ty Sub-Lt, RNVR
Lincoln, Albert Harry	Ty Lt (E) RNVR
Lockwood, William Keith	Ty Sub-Lt (A) RNVR
Monks, Newton Lee Ponting	Ty Pay Sub-Lt RNR
Moore, Thomas J A	Ty Sub-Lt (E) RNR
Paden, Richard	Ty Sub-Lt (A) RNVR
Scotchmoor, John William	Ty Lt Cdr (E) RNR
Stallard-Penoyre, Ralph Carnac Baker	Lieutenant RN
Storey, Thomas Pollard, DSC	Ty Surg Lt RNVR
Swan, William Arthur	Ty Act Sub-Lt (E) RNVR

Tetlow, Frank	Ty Act Sub-Lt (E) RNVR
Walker, John Russel	Ty Sub-Lt (A) RNVR
Wrathall, John Sandford	Ty Act Lt RNVR

Missing Presumed Killed

Abrahams, Cyril J	Air Mechanic 2nd Class	FAA/FX.83180
Acott, Frank A G	Ordinary Seaman	C/JX.376489
Allan, William F	Steward	D/LX.26746
Allen, Arthur E	Telegraphist	C/JX.149039
Allen, Bernard	Able Seaman	C/JX.301148
Almond, Eric	Ordinary Seaman	P/JX.372307
Anderson, Alexander	Ordinary Seaman	C/JX.372884
Anderson, George S	Air Mechanic 2nd Class	FAA/FX.81026
Anstruther, David R	Ordinary Seaman	D/JX.348819
Arslett, Frederick J	Air Mechanic (E) 1st Class	FAA/SFX.2476
Atherton, Charles E	Able Seaman	C/JX.260436
Ayers, Stanley	Carpenter's Mate	T.124.X
Bailey, John W	Signalman	C/JX.309419
Baker, Valentine J	Yeoman Signals (Ty) R.F.R.	C/J.107758
Barnes, William	Able Seaman	C/JX.238822
Bartley, Ernest S	Ordinary Telegraphist	C/JX.341560
Barwise, John H	Able Seaman	C/JX.259141
Batchelor, Jack H	Air Mechanic (L) 1st Class	FAA/SFX.2517
Baylis, Michael V	Signalman	C/JX.344709
Bennett, Jack D	Ordinary Seaman	C/JX.332202
Bevin, Gordon A	Ordinary Coder	C/JX.344942
Bingham, George C	Able Seaman	C/JX.319257
Bland, Ivan H	Ordinary Seaman	C/JX.355221
Bloomfield, Leonard W	Ldg Radio Mechanic (AW)	FAA/FX.100747
Boag-Jones, Dennis P	Air Mechanic (A) 1st Class	FAA/FX.82212
Bond, Douglas A	Ordinary Signalman	C/JX.344711
Botton, Norman D	Leading Supply Assistant (Ty)	C/MX.69527
Bottril, Cuthbert L	Able Seaman	C/JX.303407
Bowles, George B	Scullion	T.124.X
Bowman, Horace E	Ldg Radio Mechanic(AW)	FAA/FX.82231
Boyle, Francis	Able Seaman	C/JX.312325

Bramhall, Edward L	Diesel Greaser	T.124.X
Bramwell, Reginald R	Ordinary Seaman	C/JX.351198
Brandreth, James	Assistant Cook	T.124.X
Bretherton, Thomas F	Able Seaman	C/SSX.36069
Brett, Dennis G	Air Mechanic (O) 1st Class	FAA/SFX.1499
Brown, Alexander M	Ordinary Seaman	C/JX.376796
Brown, Clifford T B	Leading Seaman (Ty)	C/JX.151184
Brown, John H	Air Fitter (O)	FAA/FX.77765
Brown, Robert B	Able Seaman	P/JX.266654
Bryant, Daniel W	Ldg Telegraphist.RNV(W)	RC/WRX.139
Burls, Frank C	Able Seaman	C/JX.190291
Burness, Albert E	Acting Able Seaman	C/SSX.34144
Bursey, Graham	Able Seaman	C/JX.246665
Bush, John R	Leading Seaman (Ty)	C/JX.145580
Buswell, Peter E V	Air Mechanic (A) 1st Class	FAA/FX,83909
Butler William A	Able Seaman	C/JX.277273
Butterfield, Joseph N	Able Seaman	C/JX.279269
Byrne, David E	Able Seaman	C/JX.225994
Caldow, Robert	Ordinary Seaman	C/JX.352223
Campbell, John C	Acting Able Seaman	C/JX.262397
Candlish, William	Able Seaman	C/JX.237543
Capstick, Joseph A	Chief Petty Officer Telegraphist	C/J.46054
Carrat, Walter	Able Seaman	C/JX.199849
Carter, Harold O	Yeoman of Signals Ty.	C/SSX.17317
Casson, William E A	Acting Able Seaman	C/JX.197543
Castle, Rex	Assistant Steward	D/LX.29115
Chaplin, George W B	Chief Petty Officer A F (E)	FAA/F.55010
Chappel, Ronald A	Assistant Steward	T.124.X
Clark, Arthur S	Air Mechanic (E) 2nd Class	FAA/FX.86308
Clark, William E	Leading Seaman Ty.	C/JX.160256
Clauson, William D	Able Seaman	C/SSX.23479
Clayton, James	Leading Seaman Ty.	C/JX.142952
Clements, Kenneth G	Leading Steward	T.124.X
Cluett, William G	Air Mechanic (O) 1st Class	FAA/FX.86307
Cockerell, Leslie H	Acting Able Seaman	C/JX.248813
Comber, Alfred J	Able Seaman	P/J.94507

Combstock, Frederick J	Ordinary Seaman	D/JX.347470
Congdon, Noel C E	Ordinary Seaman	P/JX.357886
Cooley, Reginald D	Ldg Radio Mechanic (AW)	FAA/FX.87765
Corral, Noel L	Able Seaman	C/JX.319290
Coulson, George V T	Able Seaman	C/JX.148891
Cox, Frederick J	Assistant Steward	T.124.X
Crooks, Ivor E	Ordinary Seaman	C/JX.379344
Cunningham, Albert	Able Seaman RNVR	C/LDX.2494
Dando, Edwin J	Acting Leading Airman (Ty)	FAA/SFX.2864
Davis, Stanley	Leading Seaman Ty.	C/JX.225276
Davison, Edward H	Able Seaman	C/JX.168959
Dawson, Albert J B	Leading Air Mechanic (L)	FAA/SFX.628
Day, Frederick G W	Able Seaman RNVR	C/LDX.5093
Devlin, John	Carpenter's Mate	T.124X.
Dickson, William	Leading Steward	T.124.X
Diggins, John H	Able Seaman	C/JX.193568
Donoghue, Sydney T	Able Seaman	C/JX.224628
Dowd, Thomas A	Petty Officer	C/JX.147634
Edwards, Augustus	Able Seaman	C/JX.201321
Fahey, John T	Acting Able Seaman	P/JX.321159
Falla, Lesley L	Ordinary Telegraphist	C/JX.271799
Farley, William G	Assistant Cook	T.124.X
Farthing, Ronald A	Assistant Cook	T.124.X
Ferneyhough, Wilfred	Able Seaman	C/JX.189663
Fisher, Albert S	Electrical Artificer	C/SR.8276
Fitzgerald, Anthony	Able Seaman	C/JX.220913
Flanagan, Dennis	Diesel Greaser	T.124.X
Flower, Kenneth H	Acting Petty Officer AM. (O)	FAA/FX.77086
Fox, George E	Air Mechanic (A) 1st Class	FAA/FX.79161
French, William E P	Stoker 1st Class	C/KX.105295
Fulker, Henry C	Air Mechanic (E)	FAA/FX.92524
Furrell, Patrick R	Supply Petty Officer	C/MX.52485
Gamble, John M	Ldg Radio Mechanic (AR)	FAA/FX.88200
Gibson, John A	Carpenter's Mate	T.124.X
Gibson, Roy	Acting Able Seaman	C/JX.316841
Gilbert, James W	Ordinary Seaman	C/JX.317966

Gilroy, James	Able Seaman	C/JX.315140
Goswell, Richard F	RPO (DNA SC 8222/43)	C/M.40032
Gray, Archibald	Boatswain	T.124.X
Griffin, Bertie W	Able Seaman	P/JX.316118
Griffiths, Charles W	Diesel Greaser	T.124.X
Griffiths, William R	Air Fitter (E)	FAA/SFX.2042
Gunner, Frederick J	Able Seaman	C/JX.195146
Habgood, George A	Butcher 1st Class	T.124.X
Hambrook, Robert F	Chief Yeoman of Signals	C/J.110579
Hampton, Thom F	Able Seaman	W/SSX.13594
Handley, Donald C	Ldg Radio Mechanic (AR)	FAA/JX.357091
Handley, John G	Acting Ldg Air Mechanic (E)	FAA/SFX.264
Handy, Ernest H	Petty Officer	C/JX.134868
Harrop, Thomas	Air Fitter (E)	FAA/FX.83023
Hart, Henry	Donkeyman	T.124.X
Hartill, Horace	Naval Airman 2nd Class	FAA/FX.93960
Harvey, Clayton W A	Able Seaman	C/JX.316615
Harvey, William J	Able Seaman	C/JX.279344
Haskayne, James A	Ldg Radio Mechanic (AW)	FAA/FX.82981
Hicks, Joseph	Air Mechanic (E) 1st Class	FAA/FX.84551
Hill, James O T	Able Seaman	C/JX.316502
Hill, Joseph	Ship's Cook	T.124.X
Hind, Bert J	Air Mechanic (O) 1st Class	FAA/FX.92579
Hobbs, Joseph F	Able Seaman	C/JX.278289
Hodkinson, Percy C	Telegraphist	C/JX.178427
Hodkinson, Peter	Ldg Radio Mechanic	P/MX.102049
Horne, John R	Sick Berth Attendant	C/MX.85545
Horne, Sylvester R A J	Air Mechanic (E) 1st Class	FAA/FX.83836
Howse, Leslie G T	Photographer (A)	FAA/MX.101858
Hoyle, Laurence	Leading Air Fitter (E)	FAA/SFX.2913
Humphreys, Albert	Leading Seaman Ty.	C/JX.127052
Hurst, Frederick M	Ship's Cook	T.124.X
Inglesfield, Joseph	Able Seaman	C/JX.333162
Ingram, Dennis A	Assistant Steward	T.124.X
Irvine, George B	Supply Assistant	P/MX.82797
Jackson, Henry R	Leading Airman Ty	FAA/FX.87319

Jackson, Leonard	Acting Able Seaman	C/JX.315182
Jackson, Stephen	Baker 1st Class	T.124.X
Jeffrey, Andrew	Diesel Greaser	T.124.X
Jennings, Nelson P	Able Seaman	C/LDX.4789
Johnson, Harold W	Ordinary Signalman	C/JX.298702
Joy, Edwin G	Air Mechanic(A) 1st Class	FAA/FX.84427
Kemp, Oscar C	Petty Officer	C/JX.130904
Kenah, John E	Able Seaman	C/JX.279071
Kennedy, William	Able Seaman	C/JX.182786
Keverne, Richard H J	Acting Petty Officer Air Mechanic (O)	
		FAA/FX.77087
Kilburn, William	Chief Steward 1st Class	T.124.X
Kilpatrick, Samuel J	Able Seaman	P/JX.306997
Knowles, Frank	Able Seaman	C/JX.319685
Kyle, Charles Mc	Able Seaman	C/JX.289245
Langston, Enos J	Air Mechanic (E) 1st Class	FAA/FX.82213
Levick, Roy E	Acting Ldg Air Mechanic (E)	FAA/FX.76058
Lewis, Alan W G	Assistant Steward	T.124.X
Lightwing, James A	Ordinary Seaman	C/JX.374404
Linfield, William S L	Able Seaman	C/JX.247986
Loade, William	Steward	D/LX.26017
Lonsdale, Cyril	Air Mechanic (O) 2nd Class	FAA/FX.94533
Luffingham, Arthur	Able Seaman	C/SSX.15239
Lumby, Arthur	Ldg Radio Mechanic (AW)	FAA/FX.87283
MacAulay, Hugh	Ordinary Seaman	C/JX.316449
McCann, Joseph	Air Mechanic (E) 1st Class	FAA/SFX.906
McCarthy, Daniel	Able Seaman	C/JX.201329
McCarthy, Victor D	Able Seaman	C/JX.195151
McCracken, Peter W	Naval Airman 2nd Class	FAA/FX.90055
McLean, Walter	Ordinary Seaman	C/JX.352453
McLellan, John	Air Mechanic 2nd Class	FAA/FX.84560
McMurray, John P	Naval Airman 2nd Class	FAA/FX.101282
McSwain, James M	Leading Seaman	D/J.27914
Mahon, James T	Able Seaman	C/JX.173315
Mahon, William	Air Mechanic (O) 1st Class	FAA/FX.84092
Mahoney, Edward J	Air Mechanic (L) 1st Class	FAA/SFX.2430

Maidment, Walter J	Diesel Greaser	T.124.X
Mainland, James S	Acting Ldg Air Mechanic (L)	FAA/SFX.612
Marson, William	Able Seaman	C/JX.316912
Marston, Henry C	Able Seaman	C/JX.300111
Mason, Henry S	Ordinary Telegraphist	C/JX.250509
Mason, William C	Leading Supply Assistant (Ty)	C/MX.84090
Maxted, Jack	Assistant Cook	T.124.X
Maxwell, Robert	Air Mechanic (A) 1st Class	FAA/FX.80667
Milsted, William H	Ordinary Seaman	C/JX.331451
Mitchell, David J	Leading Supply Assistant (Ty)	C/MX.94654
Mollett, Henry G	Ordinary Seaman	C/JX.353724
Moody, George E	Leading Seaman (Ty)	C/JX.133401
Moody, Joseph H	Acting Leading Airman (Ty)	FAA/FX.89609
Moore, John R	Air Mechanic 2nd Class	FAA/SR.317
Morgan, Frederick A	Able Seaman	C/JX.137744
Morgan, John J	Leading Seaman	P/JX.186173
Mosey, Walter	Able Seaman	C/SSX.25471
Moss, Alexander M	Saloon Steward	T.124.X
Mouland, John H L	Acting Ldg Air Mechanic (E)	FAA/SFX.1242
Mudd, Horace H	Acting Able Seaman	P/JX.315913
Mullins, James	Air Mechanic 2nd Class	FAA/FX.89500
Murton, Norman	Sick Berth Petty Officer (Ty)	C/MX.49288
Neighbour, Thomas H	Able Seaman	C/JX.299146
Nethercott, Henry E	Steward	D/LX.26845
Nichol, Wilfred J	Carpenter's Mate	T.124.X
Nicholson, Albert J	Able Seaman	C/JX.240864
Norman, Frank	Air Mechanic (A) 1st Class	FAA/SFX.2593
Norton, John B	Signalman	C/JX.148936
Nunn, Arthur D	Air Mechanic (E) 1st Class	FAA/FX.83693
Oakman, Stanley	Ordinary Seaman	C/JX.315571
O'Brien, Arnold	Ordinary Seaman	C/JX.353051
O'Connnor, Francis J	Able Seaman	C/JX.279101
O'Donnel, John	Cleaner	T.124.X
O'Malley, Charles E	Cleaner	T.124.X
O'Neil, John	Fireman	T.124.X
Oxford, William A	Fireman	T.124.X

Paice, Reginal E	Air Mechanic (O) 2nd Class	FAA/FX.94546
Parkinson, Donald	Air Mechanic (L) 1st Class	FAA/SFX.2616
Paterson, James R	Assistant Baker	T.124.X
Paxton, George W	Leading Air Fitter (A)	FAA/FX.83231
Peet, Joseph D O	Air Fitter (O)	FAA/FX.82416
Pell, Fred	Leading Airman (Ty)	FAA/JX.193497
Petty, Charles J	Able Seaman	C/JX.278463
Phillibrown, Harry C	Ordinary Seaman	C/JX.374889
Pigden, Charles F	Ordinary Seaman	C/JX.374891
Pitman, Peter E V	1st Writer	T.124.X
Pile, Stephen G	Petty Officer	C/J.101696
Plant, Percy H	Able Seaman	C/JX.283544
Playford, Cyril E	Able Seaman	C/JX.160947
Potter, Lawrence	Assistant Steward	T.124.X
Price, Percy D	Stoker 1st Class	C/KX.90532
Rayward, Clifford	Air Mechanic (O) 1st Class	FAA/JX.231349
Reed, Robert	Ordinary Seaman	C/JX.352493
Reeves, John	Petty Officer Air Fitter (O)	FAA/FX.80136
Reid, Allan	Cleaner	T.124.X
Richardson, George T	Petty Officer Air Fitter (O)	FAA/FX.79940
Richardson, Harry	Able Seaman	C/JX.171624
Richardson, William	Storekeeper 1st Class	T.124.X
Richer, Jack	Able Seaman	D/J.59908
Rix, Richard D	Ordinary Seaman	C/JX.353084
Roberts, Dennis	Mechanic	T.124.X
Roberts, Geoffrey	Air Fitter (A)	FAA/FX.86050
Roberts, Peter	Leading Telegraphist	C/JX.143601
Robinson, William J	Saloon Steward	T.124.X
Robson, James	Acting Able Seaman	C/JX.314025
Rockliff, John	Ordinary Seaman	C/JX.354227
Rodway, Harry	Air Mechanic (O) 2nd Class	FAA/FX.94665
Rogerson, Norman J	Air Mechanic (E) 1st Class	FAA/FX.82785
Rolph, Alfred J	Stoker 1st Class	C/KX.104771
Ross, Henry	Air Mechanic (A) 1st Class	FAA/FX.83784
Ross, Henry	Painter	T.124.X
Routley, Harold G	Acting Petty Officer Air Mechanic (E)	

		FAA/FX.76574
Salmon, John T	Leading Steward (Ty)	D/LX.24940
Salter, Samuel J	Air Mechanic (E) 1st Class	FAA/FX.83109
Scanlon, Thomas	Able Seaman	C/JX.237014
Schooling, Joseph R	Acting Ldg Air Mechanic (L)	FAA/FX.76644
Scott, William H	Able Seaman	C/JX.172434
Scragg, Francis H	Acting Air Artificer 4th Class	FAA/FX.75576
Seward, Leslie A	Able Seaman	C/JX.161731
Sharpe, William C	Able Seaman	C/JX.199851
Sheldon, Horace V	Sick Berth Attendent	C/MX.94630
Sheppard, John A	Ordinary Seaman	C/JX.374470
Shirley, Edward W	Leading Air Fitter (L)	FAA/FX.75535
Shuttleworth, George W	Air Mechanic (A) 1st Class	FAA/SFX.1037
Simmonds, Arthur S	Air Mechanic (L) 1st Class	FAA/FX.80985
Simpson, Dennis W	Air Mechanic (A) 1st Class	FAA/FX.84460
Skinner, Leslie R	Leading Telegraphist	C/SSX.16331
Slade, John	Diesel Greaser	T.124.X
Smith, Ernest F	Photographer (A)	FAA/MX.93131
Smith, Leslie D	Ordnance Artificer 4th Class	C/MX.76076
Sneddon, William B	Air Mechanic (L) 1st Class	FAA/FX.79517
Snell, Ivan	Air Mechanic (O) 1st Class	FAA/SFX.2335
Spence, Alexander P M	Able Seaman	C/SSX.21966
Speirs, William A	Signalman	C/JX.309405
Sporton, Albert V H	Ordinary Seaman	P/JX.324724
Spratt, Rodney N	Able Seaman	C/JX.199797
Stamp, John A	Petty Officer RNVR	C/TD/X.909
Stanton, Roy L	Able Seaman	P/JX.323583
Stead, Wilfred	Ldg Radio Mechanic (AR)	FAA/FX.88236
Stockford, Albert J	Air Mechanic (O) 2nd Class	FAA/FX.85689
Sullivan, Thomas	Electrical Artificer 2nd Class	C/MX.46283
Sweetnam, Cuthbert B	Supply Assistant	D/MX.107019
Tallack, Richard J	Air Artificer 4th Class	FAA/SFX.344
Taylor, Cyril G	Ordinary Seaman	C/JX.327124
Taylor, Frederick J	Greaser	T.124.X
Tennant, Herbert W	Assistant Storekeeper	T.124.X
Terrey, Cyril J	Petty Officer Telegraphist	C/JX.134049

Thistle, Cyril R	Able Seaman	C/JX.315756
Thompson, James	Able Seaman	C/SSX.18878
Thomson, Alexander MA	Naval Airman 2nd Class	FAA/FX.98233
Thornhill, Raymond	Able Seaman	C/JX.318466
Tickner, William T	Acting Radio Petty Officer (Ty)	C/J.109099
Timmis, Robert	Able Seaman	C/SSX.24437
Tinto, Leslie G	Scullion	T.124.X
Tomblin, William J R	Coder	C/JX.293104
Tordoff, Dennis A	Carpenter's Mate	T.124.X
Tosh, William	Assistant Steward	T.124.X
Travis, William	Storekeeper	T.124.X
Turner, Eric R	Air Mechanic (O) 2nd Class	FAA/FX.94452
Turner, Frank O	Leading Seaman	C/SSX.20187
Varcoe, Jack	Assistant Steward	D/LX.26736
Vaughan, George	Assistant Cook	T.124.X
Voice, Stanley C	Leading Air Fitter (A)	FAA/FX.81775
Wain, George W	Leading Air Mechanic (O)	FAA/SFX.144
Walker, John C	Able Seaman	C/JX.169472
Walsh, Thomas	Assistant Steward	T.124.X
Webb, Joseph H	Naval Airman 2nd Class	FAA/FX.94804
Whittington, Richard A	Able Seaman	C/JX.173033
Williams, Dennis R	Air Mechanic (O) 1st Class	FAA/FX.84125
Williams, Robert	Air Mechanic (E) 1st Class	FAA/FX.90025
Willis, Howard	Air Mechanic (O) 2nd Class	FAA/FX.94483
Wood, George	Fireman	T.124.X
Woodward, Claude	Air Mechanic (O) 1st Class	FAA/FX.81670
Woolley, Henry G	Chief Petty Officer	C/J.105610
Worsdell, Albert C	Ordinary Seaman	P/JX.345517
Yates, Thomas	Able Seaman	C/JX.168689
Young, Albert J	Petty Officer Airman	FAA/F.55142
Young, Cecil A	Able Seaman	C/JX.316666

N.A.A.F.I.
Missing Presumed Killed

Cowen, David	Canteen Manager
Shearer, James D	Canteen Assistant
Webb, Victor	Leading Canteen Assistant

Royal Air Force Personnel

Grieve, Alexander	Flight Sergeant	564019

Missing Presumed Killed

Leonard, Roger	Sergeant	523319
Parks, Stanley Muirson	Corporal	533572

Commander EWE Lane was the most senior officer to give evidence to the board of enquiry investigating the loss of HMS Dasher. *The board convened three days after the disaster on board the sister ship HMS* Archer, *anchored off Greenock. Like all witnesses called, after he had given his evidence Commander Lane was ordered not to speak about the loss of the ship*

ASSESSING THE EVIDENCE

The day following the disaster, Vice Admiral GLSG Diptin summoned two commanders and three captains to 'Hold a full and careful investigation into the circumstances attending the loss of HMS *Dasher*.' The president of the board was to be Captain Guy Grantham CB DSO, HMS *Indomitable*.

His board consisted of Commander R Cobb OBE, HMS *Indomitable*; Commander HD McMaster, HMS *Archer*; Captain JR Robertson, HMS *Archer*; and Captain RG Holt, Staff of Commander-in-Chief Home Fleet.

The board assembled on board HMS *Archer*, which was anchored at the Tail o' the Bank, Greenock and the board of enquiry commenced at 9.30am on Tuesday 30th March.

After suffering the loss of their ship, with many of their shipmates still on board, witnessing the suffering and terrible deaths of scores of the crew to the searing flames in the water, twenty five of the survivors were taken out from Greenock in an open boat to a sister ship of *Dasher*. As the open boat made its way to the aircraft carrier HMS *Archer*, the twenty five survivors of *Dasher* must have suffered further trauma as they were looking up at an almost identical ship to the one that had sunk three days previously.

The minutes of the board of enquiry make very interesting reading. They consist of five hundred and sixty questions being asked of thirty four witnesses who were not represented, legally or otherwise. Many of the questions were asked in a brisk fashion. Innuendo and doubt were also cast.

Surprisingly, no witnesses were called from the two coastal vessels, the *Lithium* and the *Cragsman*, who between them saved half of the survivors. Of the countless witnesses to the whole tragic event on the coast of Ayrshire and Arran, not one was called to give vital evidence.

Perhaps even more surprising, Captain LAK Boswell and navigating officer, (later Captain) AP Culmer, two of *Dasher's* most senior officers, were not called to give evidence.

The first witness to be called was Commander EWE Lane. As with all witnesses, he was placed under oath or in naval terminology, he was cautioned in accordance with KRAI, Article 488 para 9.

'Will you please explain briefly,' asked the president of the board of enquiry, Captain G Grantham, 'what you know of the circumstances of this case, to the best of your ability?' Commander Lane reported,

> 'I was in the bridge and about to write down what I was doing when the ship shuddered, aft, accompanied by a large bang, not very loud. My immediate reaction was that there had been an explosion in the engine room or boiler take-ups, as it was similar to previous explosions of that nature. I looked over the bridge and my first view was confirmation of this. Smoke and small black objects were travelling horizontally on the starboard side. I then saw very much more smoke than we had before and further aft. The Officer of the Watch then said, 'Crikey, look at that'.
> ' 'That' was the aircraft lift in its entirety, weighing in excess of two tons and soaring fifty feet above the flight deck. It was perfectly horizontal and on reaching about sixty feet, it plummeted into the sea, portside. I then noticed considerable smoke and flames were rising from the lift opening and the flight deck was buckled up to half the after length of the hangar. On the starboard side there were two

burst places out of which smoke and flames were appearing.

'There were volumes of smoke accompanied by large tongues of flame. I went down on to the flight deck and told the hands who were standing around to run out the fire hoses. Captain Boswell called me from the bridge and asked me what had happened. I said I did not know but I would find out.

'The ship had taken a gradually increasing list to starboard down by the stern, but by the time the captain had called me the ship had returned quickly upright but trimmed by the stern. I went down to the first deck and made my way to the second deck by ladder outside the captain's cabin. I proceeded aft along the port alleyway. There were no lights but smoke and debris were there and further aft the gangway was obstructed by the galley and Chief Petty Officers' Mess, approximately 108 Station, above the engine room and about eighty feet (24 metres) forward of the petrol stowage. By this time the ship was still further down by the stern, smoke was very thick and there was a sound of rushing water and grinding metal from below and aft. I looked down a hatch outside the provision issue room, that is on 105 Station and could hear water pouring in. I saw about three feet (1 metre) of water on the third deck.

'This hatch gave me access to the engine room aft and a recreation space forward. The ship seemed to be settled aft and I made my way to the upper deck by the same route I had come. I looked in cabins and offices but they appeared to be empty by the port side. I then endeavoured to get hands to swing out the boats. Carley rafts were already being released from the walkways.

'Water was by now coming over the upper deck, level with the forward end of the hangar. I crawled forward to the port lower boom and went over the side as the ship rapidly settled by the stern until she finally became vertical and went down.'

Lieutenant Commander Wootton was then called and specifically asked questions regarding the engine room ventilation system and the petrol stowage tanks. During his replies he mentioned a leak of petrol from a petrol tank cock in the engine room. The rate of leakage was said by Commander Wootton to be 'very slow, about one drip every five seconds.'

It also emerged that as well as this 'very slow' leak from a petrol tank cock, there was another potentially even more calamitous means by which highly inflammable liquid could leak into uncontrolled areas. The enquiry board asked Commander Wootton when on one occasion the petrol stowage tanks were partially flooded and water was found leaking into the shaft tunnel, 'Were the holes into the shaft tunnel plugged?'

'No sir,' replied Commander Wootton.

'So they were in fact still open,' he was asked.

'There was one hole about one inch (25mm) in diameter. Actually it was a hole for an electric light cable but no wiring was run through it.'

The commander was recalled and asked questions on the same subjects, then recalled again to reply to further questions regarding the petrol leakage and also on access to the control room. It is interesting to note that the average number of questions each witness was asked was sixteen. Commander Wootton was asked sixty questions and at one stage he apologised to the board of enquiry for stating that the fuel tanks were empty when in fact they were full.

When Captain JH MacNair of HMS *Isle of Sark* was questioned, it was ascertained that he had ordered Full Speed to assist in the rescue operation. When asked how many survivors he picked up, he replied,

> 'We picked up thirty two and three more who were unconscious. We applied artificial respiration with the three for more than three hours. We thought that one would survive but in the end he collapsed and could not be revived.'

On being asked if the survivors were covered in oil, he replied, 'Survivors were covered in oil and difficult to get hold of.' His answer to, 'Were the survivors wearing lifebelts?' was, 'Not all of them were wearing lifebelts.'

When Petty Officer FC Lovell was asked what he felt and saw, he replied,

> 'It seemed as if the whole ship seemed to blow up, everything went into complete darkness. There was a clattering of lockers falling over and doors being blown off. I was picked up and thrown across the mess and collided with a stanchion. I scrambled out of the door and met suffocating fumes which smelt like exhaust gases. It was difficult to find my way out owing to debris, smoke and lack of light.'

As each witness was dismissed, he was instructed not to discuss the disaster. After receiving answers to 560 questions asked, the board of enquiry ended the taking of evidence. From the answers given, it became apparent that,

After the explosion there were large quantities of black smoke;

Orange and red tongues of flame were shooting from the aircraft lift shaft;

Fire spread along the tops of the fuel tanks which contained 75000 gallons of diesel;

The Fleet Air Arm central stores were shrouded in smoke and flames;

The hangar was filled with smoke and flames from a very big fire;

Many major fires spread throughout the ship;

Twenty four depth charges had been stored in the hangar, twelve feet, (4 metres) from the aircraft lift;

Sixty eight depth charges were stored forward of the aircraft lift;

Six torpedoes were stored in the hangar, warheads had been fitted and they were all facing the stern of the ship;

Aircraft in the hangar were being refuelled;

The hangar had no asbestos blankets fitted, in contravention of

> Royal Navy practice for aircraft carriers;
>
> *Dasher* was fully laden for convoy duties with ammunition for all aircraft guns, the ship's four anti-aircraft guns, four 40mm guns and the eight 20mm guns;
>
> The Fleet Air Arm crew who had just been dismissed and had adjourned to their mess deck, perished instantly, as that part of the ship took the main thrust of the explosion.

It is interesting at this distance of time to consider the conduct of the board of enquiry from a psychological perspective. After the tragic events and great loss of life, it was indeed necessary to carry out a full enquiry to ascertain how the disaster occurred. From our modern day standpoint however, it would be a matter of deep concern for the enquiry to be carried out on a sister ship of HMS *Dasher*, a vessel almost identical to the stricken ship.

Survivors of the tragedy who were in fact surviving victims, would in many cases be suffering the effects of what we now know as Post Traumatic Stress Disorder. This is a condition which is now well-researched and documented, but at the time was unheard of. The symptoms may occur for decades after the event and are now minimised where possible, by counselling and sensitive handling immediately after the event.

In the case of *Dasher*, the action of those in charge in organising an enquiry on a ship almost identical to the one in which the survivors were plucked from a burning sea, witnessing shipmates die around them, displays an almost unbelievable lack of the most basic sensitivity and undertsanding. The crew who were interviewed had neither legal or moral support and in certain cases were recalled to further interrogation with the implication of blame.

It would be professional psychological opinion that the experience of the interrogation aboard HMS *Archer* would act only to magnify feelings of distress, guilt and anxiety. It was a major error of judgment on the part of the Admiralty with long term ramifications for the victims.

The minutes of the *Enquiry into the loss of HMS Dasher* and the *Report of the Board of Enquiry* were looked at for a legal opinion.

There would appear to be no doubt that given the information they had to hand, the board of enquiry felt they were correct in concluding that the initial explosion was in the petrol tanks. They felt that the 'rumbling' explosion would probably be different from a detonation of high explosive.

Legal opinion formed the impression that there was on *Dasher* insufficient awareness of the dangers which could be caused by a build up of gas from the stored petrol. Fuel gas escapes from even 'liquid-tight' containers which do not have any drip from such a joint described in the evidence of Commander Wootton – 'a drip every five seconds'. Commander Wootton was considered to be rather casual in his approach to the elimination of this drip.

The findings seemed to suggest that only a lighted cigarette (or perhaps an electrical fault) could have caused the explosion, but even a spark caused by striking metal on metal could have set it off. One wonders if even the most careless of sailors would have been stupid enough to ignore No Smoking signs close to a petrol area.

One result of the *Dasher* disaster seems to have been a greater awareness of the potential danger of petroleum vapour build-up in enclosed spaces on escort carriers. One must however bear in mind that such precautions were already enforced on purpose-built aircraft carriers and that *Dasher* and her like were hastily converted in the United States from cargo ships and tankers.

One aspect of the enquiry which does bear examination is the large number of witnesses to whom the Royal Navy never ever spoke. No attempt was made to seek them out and ask them what they had experienced. If these witnesses had been called then a different picture may have emerged.

The crew on board the *City of Venice*, anchored at the entrance to Loch Long, some fifteen miles to the north, watched the dense black smoke. 'Whatever is causing the thick black smoke,' said junior engineer James Greenhill, 'must be visible to even the most casual observer. Any observer with binoculars must have seen the cause in great detail.'

James could not have spoken truer words. Unknown to him, William McAuslin, attached to the Royal Army Observer Corps, was on duty in his observation hut, situated high in the Arran hills. William made the following statement,

> 'I had been watching planes practising landings on *Dasher's* flight deck. I noticed a huge burst of smoke towards the stern. A friend who was on duty with me asked, 'Do you think she is all right?' The carrier seemed to be on an even keel when suddenly the bow started to rise out of the water. I shouted, 'Oh heavens, she is going.' As the bow rose higher in the air, a plane slid down the steeply listing flight deck and fell into the sea. The ship seemed to stand on end, then it slowly disappeared before me. I still had my binoculars trained on the spot and I saw three rafts on the surface. I counted seven or eight people on the first raft, not so many on the second and only one on the third.'

Alex Buchanan was on the bridge of the *Isle of Sark*, five miles south of *Dasher*. When the explosion was heard, they headed for the scene at full speed. As he had his camera in his hands, he took a photograph immediately of the huge thick black column of smoke. As they approached, they swung out their lifeboats in readiness.

When they were one mile from the scene, he took another photograph. By now the aircraft carrier was gone. At this point, he took a third dramatic photograph, as he could see some life rafts and survivors in the water.

On reaching the scene, they quickly lowered their lifeboats and cast off to pluck the survivors from the cold sea. Alex watched as the *Isle of Sark* crew hauled survivors and many of the deceased on board the lifeboats.

When the lifeboats returned, having ensured that they could be of no more assistance, the survivors and deceased were helped on board the *Isle of Sark*. Alex and his shipmates covered them with blankets and helped them below. *Dasher's* captain and the ship's navigator were among the thirty two saved from the cruel sea by the crew of the *Isle of Sark*.

Petty Officer John B Lawson served on *Dasher's* sister ship, HMS

Attacker. His testimony is worth recording in full. It brings into sharp focus one of the most dramatic elements of the whole event.

'I served aboard HMS *Attacker*. *Dasher* was supposed to join us in her first convoy from the States to the UK. However she developed engine trouble and some problems with the hydraulics on the aircraft lift. There were other teething troubles, so many in fact, she had to miss the convoy.

'*Attacker* and *Dasher* were involved in Operation Torch, the invasion of North Africa. The next time we saw *Dasher* was in the Clyde, 27th March 1943. We heard many stories of her being a 'jinx ship'. *Attacker* was working up for convoy duty. I was on the flight deck when we heard an almighty explosion. I looked towards the Cumbraes and saw a large column of smoke, then flames appeared. They were very big flames.

'We launched our two whalers and they rowed towards the area. Action Stations! was announced on board *Attacker* and everybody went to their respective posts. I was on duty in Damage Control in the hangar and as I made my way there I looked towards the black smoke and flames. The flames covered an area about half a mile square. Many rescue vessels were heading for the area.

'We were all very wary, thinking, was it a torpedo or a mine? Also if it could happen to *Dasher*, it could happen to us. While I was in the hangar, I kept a wary eye on the doors, in case I had to make a quick exit.

'On the whalers' return, the Officer of the Day took the oarsmen straight to the captain's office. Later signals were passed to all ships in the vicinity that, THE INCIDENT IS NOT, REPEAT NOT, TO BE SPOKEN ABOUT.

'We heard through the ship's grapevine that our whalers had picked up many survivors and transfered them to a Royal Navy vessel. Having being ordered not to speak about the disaster, we never ever spoke about it.'

In the light of what has been learned about coping with disasters in recent years, for those who survived and those who were bereaved, this order and the obedient response to it we now know was probably the worst advice to give. It certainly would have added to the burden of grief and shock experienced by all.

The experience of Sub Lt Lionel Godfrey RNVR 891 Squadron may be an object lesson in how officialdom can outface the facts in holding to the truth as they think it should be perceived. From December 1942 Lionel Godfrey was stationed as a member of the Fleet Air Arm at Machrihanish on the Mull of Kintyre. He takes up the story in his own words

'We enjoyed our short time at Machrihanish. It was always a good, hospitable place where the station officers and men welcomed our presence among them and did their best to help us relax from operational duty. Had we known what was about to happen to some of us within minutes of leaving Machrihanish none of us would have wanted to stay anywhere else but on the Mull of Kintyre.

'The day before *Dasher* took up her operational duties once more, four of our Hurricanes, their pilots and almost all of the maintenance personnel had been taken aboard by lighter as the ship swung at anchor in the Firth of Clyde. The following day Max Newman, myself and two other pilots were circling the carrier as she worked up speed into wind preparatory to us landing, when *Dasher* exploded before our very eyes and sank from view within minutes. In my mind's eye I can still see the lift being hurled some two to three hundred feet in the air and bodies falling from its surface into the sea. There was absolutely nothing that we could do except keep radio silence and return to Machrihanish where our Commanding Officer reported verbally what we had witnessed.

'891 Squadron, left with only four aircraft, four pilots and less than a dozen maintenance personnel, was disbanded almost immediately from Machrihanish. Two days later I ended up taking compulsory leave in London with no appointment or designation to another squadron or to a shore base. It was a sad end to what had been a happy association with an efficient fighter squadron. At no time since the tragic end of HMS *Dasher* have I heard of or seen an official acknowledgement of her loss.

'After four weeks leave without pay and without notice of an appointment back to duty, I visited a branch of the Admiralty in Queen Anne's Mansions, London in an endeavour to learn what I should do with myself. From a Commander seated behind a desk in a depressing looking office I received a flat denial that anything untoward had happened to *Dasher* or to 891 Squadron. When I, a mere Sub Lieutenant (A) RNVR, protested that with my own eyes I'd seen *Dasher* go down and disappear beneath the calm waters of the Firth of Clyde, the only response I got from the severe looking Commander was "Nonsense! You'd better get yourself a casual payment and remain on indefinite leave. You'll be informed when you're needed." '

CHAPTER 7

REPORT OF THE BOARD OF ENQUIRY

BOARD OF ENQUIRY HELD ON BOARD H.M.S. 'ARCHER' ON TUESDAY AND WEDNESDAY, 30TH AND 31ST MARCH 1943 TO INVESTIGATE INTO THE CIRCUMSTANCES ATTENDING

LOSS OF HMS 'DASHER' ON 27TH MARCH, 1943

SCHEDULE OF CONTENTS

SECRET.

H.M.S. 'ARCHER'
        31st March, 1943

Sir,
In accordance with your Memorandum dated 28th March, 1943, directing us to enquire into the loss of HMS 'DASHER' on the 27th March, 1943, we have the honour to submit the following report:–

2.   HMS 'DASHER' sank at approximately 1648A on 27th March in approximate position 205 degrees Cumbrae Island Light 5 miles. Commanding Officer and 148 of her ship's company survived out of a total of 527.

3.   The following facts have been established:–

(a)   Explosion was not due to any external cause.

(b)   It was a muffled rumbling report and not an instantaneous detonation.

(c)   It did not take place in the after 4" magazine; in the hangar; forward of the hangar area or in the engine room.

4.   The explosion vented itself:–

(a)   forward through the after bulkhead of the engine room low down.

(b)   upward through a large hatch just forward of the lift well.

(c)   up and out through the ship's side to starboard via the Fleet Air Arm messdeck.

(d)   presumably through the ship's bottom in one or more places.

5.   The results of the explosion were:–

(a)   Immediate failure of all light and power: emergency dynamo cut in for about 20 seconds only.

(b)   Lift, at flight deck level, blown high in the air and after end of flight deck damaged.

(c)   Violent fire at after end of hangar.

(d)   Fire in the engine room.

(e)   Rapid flooding of the ship extending from forward engine room bulkhead to the stern.

(f)   A list to starboard of not more than 10 degrees which rapidly disappeared as the ship settled quickly by the stern.

(g)   The ship sank approximately 8 minutes after the explosion.

6.   State of the ship was as follows:–

(a)   Flying had just been completed and all aircraft except one struck down.

(b)   In the hangar were 6 Swordfish and 2 Hurricanes. Two Swordfish were being fuelled.

(c)   Petrol control room was open with Greaser in attendance.

(d)   Access hatch from Fleet Air Arm messdeck to flat outside petrol control room was open.

(e)   Hatch in same flat at top of access trunk to shaft tunnel may also have been open, as this was in regular use for hourly visits to Plummer Blocks.

(f)   A hole, 1" in diameter between the shaft tunnel and main petrol compartment was known to exist.

(g)   It is uncertain whether a slow drip from a valve on one of the starboard tanks had been made good.

(h)   Some of Fleet Air Arm personnel, who had been working on aircraft and dismissed from hangar, were on their messdeck. "No smoking" notices were permanently in place above hatch to petrol control room. No sentry was placed.

(i)   Hands had been working in after depth charge stowage which is immediately abaft the petrol compartment during the forenoon. 68 depth charges were still in this magazine.

7.   We are of the opinion that:–

(I)   The original explosion took place either in the after depth charge magazine or the main petrol stowage. These two compartments are adjacent to one another.

(II)   There is no evidence that the explosion occurred in the depth charge magazine beyond the fact that this is located in the region of the explosion.

(III)   There is no direct proof that the explosion started in the main petrol stowage. But evidence shows that there may have been an accumulation of petrol vapour in the main petrol compartment and that this could have been ignited by a man smoking in the shaft tunnel, or through someone dropping a cigarette end down from the Fleet Air Arm messdeck, to the petrol control compartment or below.
It is pointed out that the lighting system is not up to magazine lighting specification, and that a fault on the system could have ignited petrol vapour when lights were switched on or off.

8.   We recommend that:–

(A)   Alterations detailed in Commander-in-Chief, Home Fleet's telegram T.O.O. 1339 of 15th February 1943 should be applied to all escort carriers at the earliest opportunity.

(B)   Access to petrol control compartments should be trunked up to the deck of the hangar, as in 'ARCHER' and in no case to a crewspace.

(C)   Until B is carried out in existing carriers, the trunk giving access to the forward end of the shaft tunnel should not be used.

(D)   The watertight door giving access from the engine room to the shaft tunnel should be permanently sealed, as had already been done in 'DASHER'.

(E)   The shaft tunnel should be fitted with a ventilating system.

(F)   All carriers to be supplied at the earliest possible moment with portable petrol detector gauges.

(G)   All carriers be instructed to carry out rigidly magazine and petrol regulations, and that all defects in petrol systems are to be reported to the Commanding Officer immediately they are discovered.

(H)   All carriers be instructed that life belts are to be worn when ships are exercising in local areas as well as at sea.

(I)   Calcium Flares should be withdrawn from carriers, but if carried should be stored in a watertight container.

9.   The behaviour and bearing of the Officers and ratings was exemplary throughout. Petty Officer STAMP R.N.V.R., assisted many young ratings to safety, but he lost his life in so doing. Petty Officer Telegraphist

TERRY displayed a similar spirit and example and was also lost.

10.   Two small coasting vessels, the S.S. 'LITHIUM' and S.S. 'CRAGSMAN' gave valuable assistance in rescuing men from the sea, working close to the oil burning on the water.

We have the honour to be,
        Sir,
Your obedient Servants, (signed)

        Captain G. Grantham C.B. D.S.O. R.N.
        (President) H.M.S. 'INDOMITABLE'

        Captain J.I. Robertson R.N.
        H.M.S. 'ARCHER'

        Constructor Captain R.G. Holt R.N.
        Staff of Commander-in-Chief, Home Fleet

        Commander R. Cobb O.B.E. R.N.
        H.M.S. 'INDOMITABLE'

        Commander H.D. McMaster R.N.R.
        H.M.S. 'ARCHER'

HMS Dasher *on the Hudson River in July 1942 having been converted from the recently launched merchant ship* Rio de Janerio

CHAPTER 8

THE SHORT LIFE OF DASHER

During 1941, enemy U-boats were attacking vital convoys and sinking many British merchant ships. The result of each sinking was catastrophic as the terrible loss was threefold. The much-needed ship was lost, the valuable cargo was lost and hundreds of merchant seamen perished.

The answer was more aircraft carriers – ships that could sail with the convoys and protect them from the dreaded wolf packs of U-boats. The time involved in building an aircraft carrier, such as the *Ark Royal* was two years. This was too long to wait. Aircraft carriers were required urgently.

The Admiralty suggested that merchant ships could be converted into fighting aircraft carriers within six months. But British merchant ships were already fully committed to the war effort and so the Admiralty ordered six aircraft carriers from United States. The six would be converted in the USA from American merchant ships.

The *Rio de Janerio* was built by the Sun Shipbuilding and Dry Dock Company in Chester, Pennsylvania and launched on April 12th 1941. She was selected for conversion by Tietjens and Lang Dry Dock Company, Brooklyn. On entering the dock, the *Rio de Janerio* was given the code letters BAVG 4. However the brass plate fitted in the bridge with the name *Rio de Janerio*, was allowed to remain.

From American merchantman to British aircraft carrier – a sectional drawing of the Archer class of carrier from 1943

1 Laundry	9 Wireless room	17 Engineers' office
2 Sick Bay	10 Photographer	18 Fans
3 Operating theatre	11 Stores	19 Captain's cabin
4 Stores	12 Hold	20 Ward room
5 Aviation stores	13 Cabins	21 Officers' galley
6 Cafeteria	14 Air fitters shop	22 Soda fountain
7 Hangar	15 Diesel engines	23 Shop
8 Cinema projector	16 Stokers' mess	24 Gyro room

25 Engineers' stores	33 Communications	41 Coding rooms
26 Stores	34 Recreation space	42 Deck offices
27 Pumps	35 Crews' mess	43 Crews' mess
28 Hold	36 Bulk stores	44 Bulk stores
29 Parachute comptmt	37 Ballast tanks	45 Hold
30 Passage	38 Loud hailer	46 Ballast
31 Cabins	39 Commander (F)	47 Passages
32 Quarter deck	40 Bridge	48 Stores

During the work, many of the ship's future crew were posted to New York to familiarise themselves with the vessel. Ordinary Coder Andrew Cockle, from Greenock, was posted to Flushing Barracks, New York and Sub Lt John Ferrier, also from Greenock, was posted to the Barbizon Plaza Hotel. The crew arrived from all parts of Britain and they all enjoyed New York hospitality to the full. Coming from a wartime environment with the blackouts the bombings and food rationing, the bright lights and neon signs of Times Square and Broadway were enjoyed by all, along with the plentiful and varied supply of food which were delights to the British matelot.

The United Services Organisation provided tickets for shows, concerts and sports events. The Stage Door Canteen served coffee and snacks, many served by actors and actresses including Broadway and Hollywood stars, some of whom also provided cabaret acts in between serving the British personnel.

BAVG 4 was taking shape. The cranes, derricks and funnel had been removed, having been replaced with a wooden flight deck, 410 feet in length, 82 feet shorter than the length of the ship.

Below deck, the accommodation for the *Rio de Janerio*'s crew of 38, had been increased to accommodate over 500 ship's personnel. Store rooms were being constructed for lifejackets, ammunition, torpedoes, depth charges, food, and clothing. Wash rooms, showers, toilets, a cinema, a first aid post and an operating theatre were also fitted. All this and much much more was required to convert the former banana boat into a floating airfield.

The British six month forecast was reduced to three months by the Americans. To prove their point that the conversion could be completed quicker, the ship was swarmed with a workforce of men and women – carpenters, welders, plumbers, electricians, painters, engineers, and cleaners. The army of tradesmen and tradeswomen worked around the clock, seven days a week.

Coupled with a workforce of hundreds and the general mêlée of the conversion, the crew were trying to organise the working of a ship in preparation for the take-over date of July 2nd 1942. To add to the total congestion, four aircraft from the Fleet Air Arm were due to arrive. Prior to the aircraft landing on the ship, the personnel who maintain the planes boarded. These included engine mechanics, air frame fitters, armaments air crew and store men. With them they brought their boxes of tools, spare engines, spare wheels, ammunition and countless other aircraft spare parts. During their attempt to store the aircraft spares they were hampered by the shipyard workforce and the ship's crew preparing for sea trials.

When the main engines were started up for the first time, a severe explosion occurred in the exhaust gas trunking and thick black smoke billowed out from underneath the flight deck. In late June the pre-acceptance trials took place with a local navigator in charge. During these trials the ship ran aground in the Hudson River.

During the trials on 1st July 1942, it was noted that the ship was not seaworthy, the conversion was incomplete and there were recurring problems with the engine and the aircraft lift. However the next evening, the official ceremony took place as planned with the Royal Navy and the American Navy represented by high ranking senior officers. The Stars and Stripes were replaced by the White Ensign and the Union Flag. A banquet dinner was held with generous servings of top quality food. The finest of wines were enhanced by being served in silver goblets. The celebration came to an end with all present toasting the success of *Dasher*, now on lease-lend from USA to Britain.

The ship's commander over this initial period, Vice-Admiral R Bell-Davies VC who had come back from retirement to active service, was succeeded by Captain CN Lentaignes DSO.

Orders were received that *Dasher* would join a convoy which would depart in August for the UK. In readiness for convoy duties the ship was put through her sea trials. However the 8,000 horse power Sun Droxford engine was still presenting serious problems. Little did the engine room personnel know that the engine would present 'machinery defects' on every voyage and put all their ability and experience to the utmost test.

Dasher was moved to the Brooklyn Navy Yard where attempts were made to overcome the engine failure. However on sea trial runs, the engine backfired frequently with shattering explosions. On one occasion pieces were seen to fly out of the exhaust vents.

Dasher's Chief Engineer had no faith in the design of the Sun Droxford engine and his opinion was not changed when, due to persistent 'machinery defects', *Dasher* failed to sail with the convoy.

Four Swordfish of 837 Squadron embarked from Jamaica where they had formed and worked up. Unfortunately on its first attempt at landing on *Dasher*, aircraft number DK763 crashed over the side of the ship.

The arrival of the aircraft coincided with another attempt to join an assembled convoy and when an attempt was made to start *Dasher*'s engine, it misfired with a loud explosion and an emmision of thick black smoke. A second attempt was made which produced a bigger explosion and more thick black smoke, much to the embarassment of the US Navy workforce. At the third attempt the engines did start. With no time being lost, the ship sailed at full speed through Long Island Sound. On passing the Statue of Liberty, many of the crew went out on deck to have a last look at New York and to have their photograph taken.

Dasher joined the convoy at Boston and departed in convoy for Halifax on August 30th, 1942. During her maiden voyage to Britain which lasted eleven days, no encounter with the enemy took place, proving that the U-boat Kapitans were wary of convoys with aircraft carriers in their presence.

The convoy arrived safely in the Clyde on September 10th. *Dasher*, like all the other American-built aircraft carriers, required modifications to the fuel storage tanks and the ammunition magazines. During the three weeks in which the ship was being modified, most of the crew were allowed shore leave.

At the completion of modification work, *Dasher* moved out to the Clyde estuary. On October 15th 1942, Sea Hurricanes and Swordfish aircraft from 891 Squadron 'landed-on'. Ten days later, Sea Hurricanes from 804 Squadron 'landed-on'. Both Squadrons took part in intensive practice of anti-submarine bombing, high altitude dive bombing, depth charge practice and dummy attacks on ships.

During the training exercises, flying accidents occurred, including crash landings. When an accident did occur, Acting

Operation Torch, the Allied invasion of North Africa, was the first taste of action for the crew of HMS Dasher. *The photograph above is of the convoy en route to Gibraltar*

Leading Airman Joseph (Joe) H Moody would always be heard to say, 'I do wish something exciting would happen to me!' Little did Joe realise that five months later, something exciting would happen that would cost him his life.

When the crew of *Dasher* started returning from leave, there was an expectancy of 'something big about to take place'. During the short time they had been on leave, an armada of Royal Navy ships including troop ships and supply ships, had gathered at the Tail o' the Bank and the nearby Holy Loch. Ships were also converging at Loch Ewe, Liverpool and Scapa Flow. Packet after packet of Top Secret orders arrived, all marked with the date and time of opening.

On the appointed day, at the precise hour, the secret orders were opened by the captains to reveal, 'OPERATION TORCH, THE ALLIED INVASION OF NORTH AFRICA.'

Dasher sailed from the Clyde on 27th October, as part of Force LX, a purely naval force consisting of the cruisers *Jamaica* and *Delhi*, four escorts and the aircraft carrier *Argus*. Force LX joined up with a huge convoy of over forty ships, comprising liners, merchant ships and Royal Navy escorts.

The convoy arrived safely at the Straights of Gibraltar and it was here that *Dasher* suffered from more engine defects. The ship was forced to reduce speed while the engine room personnel, utilising all their skill, worked as fast as they possibly could to rectify the problem. Their efforts were well rewarded as the ship picked up speed to be in her appointed position.

4am on November 8th, 1942 was zero hour for the assault landings and the launch of the first major Allied combined operation of the war. A heavy bombardment took place and as the massive invasion of thousands of troops commenced, *Dasher* launched six Sea Hurricanes of 804 Squadron. Their mission was to escort and defend an air attack on La Senia Airfield, Oran. This air attack was of prime importance to the operation as it would curtail enemy aircraft involvement when the United States troops made their sea-borne landings on the east and west coast of Oran.

Unable to find the ship on their return, because of haze, three of the aircraft made forced landings ashore. The other two were lost with their pilots. The sixth plane was involved in a dogfight with four Vichy French Devoitines (aircraft of a similar design to the RAF Spitfire). The lone Hurricane, from 804 squadron, tried to out-manoeuvre the attacking Devoitines and at the same time headed towards the open sea and the safety of HMS *Dasher*. This was not to be, as one of the Vichy French fighters managed to land some shots into the engine of the Hurricane as it dodged at low level. With the engine pouring black smoke and losing power rapidly, the pilot had no choice but to land his Hurricane in an inglorious fashion on enemy held soil, where he was taken captive.

Soon after daybreak some ships of the Vichy French fleet sailed from Oran harbour and a battle took place with Allied destroyers. As *Dasher* was at risk, she was ordered to sail close to HMS *Rodney* so as to have the protection of her massive guns.

On completion of the huge invasion and after a short stopover in Gibraltar for engine repairs, *Dasher* returned to the United Kingdom with an Operation Torch convoy. On arrival at Liverpool repairs to her main engine were carried out and the Air Direction Room was enlarged. Further modifications, prompted by the loss of her sister ship, HMS *Avenger*, were made to her bomb room.

During *Dasher*'s modification in Liverpool, an armistice was signed on November 11th and hostilities ceased throughout Algeria and Morocco. Admiral Cunningham addressed the following message to captains of all assault ships involved in the invasion. The message read,

> 'The part played by the ships composing the initial convoys was vital to the operation which has culminated in an armistice being signed. There was a phase when its success or failure rested on the captains of the assault ships. Reports of the able way in which these ships were handled throughout difficult and unfamiliar proceedings have reached me from all sides.
>
> 'I send captains, officers and crew my thanks and wish them God speed.'

During December, the crew organised an on-board Christmas party for some of the Liverpool children. When it was brought to their attention that a WREN camp was nearby, an invitation was extended and accepted by a number of Wrens who were entertained on board.

Dasher spent Christmas in Alexandria Dock, Liverpool and remained there until January 1943. After embarking aircraft, the ship sailed for the Clyde, to work-up for Arctic convoy duties. Flying exercises were also carried out and for many of the pilots, their observers and telegraphist air gunners, this was their first real landing onto an aircraft carrier.

The following month, *Dasher* had a very rough journey through the Minches before arriving at Scapa Flow, anchorage for the Home Fleet and other major units of the Royal Navy. The bleak and desolate Scapa Flow, within the Orkney Islands off the north coast of Scotland, was a natural harbour defended by over 300 anti-aircraft guns. A few days later, the ship sailed to Loch Ewe, where she joined JW53 convoy which departed on 15th February – destination Murmansk, north Russia.

The convoy was so massive, the Royal Navy protection force comprised twenty eight ships. Those on board each vessel were all too well aware of the danger associated with the forthcoming voyage as the enemy had already sunk over half a million tons of Allied shipping in the Atlantic. For convoy JW53, danger would not be from the enemy. Atrocious weather was going to be against them. Two days into the voyage the convoy encountered a force eleven gale. Waves over sixty feet high (18 metres), a wind force of 75mph and a temperature of minus 25° Fahrenheit were experienced, as well as snow squalls and severe icing conditions. The convoy was heading straight into one of the worst recorded storms that the north Atlantic had produced during the war.

So severe was the storm that six merchant ships turned back and HMS *Sheffield* had a gun turret roof smashed away by the heavy seas. *Dasher*, having been initially purpose-built to ply the coastal waters of America, was ill-equipped and was tossed about like a small cork in the crashing waves.

Petty Officer Brian A Phillpot, an aircrew member of 837 Squadron, relates,

'The storm force winds were lethal, both to the ship and to the aircraft, with the port-side taking the brunt of the extremely savage conditions. Lifeboats and Carley rafts were slowly but systematically whipped from their stowage positions and reduced to total wrecks, or vanished completely. Speed continued to be maintained and the ship's motion was so chaotic that most of the crew, in particular, air crew, speculated that she was heading for a certain capsize and very soon at that. Few people were capable of performing their normal duties and food was of little interest to the vast majority.

'All hands were called to the flight deck on our second night at sea, for the purpose of securing the wires lashing three aircraft to the deck, to try to prevent further damage to the others. The ship's pitching and rolling, coupled with the storm force winds had strained the securing wires to breaking point and since the aircraft had begun to move about, it became a matter of urgency to rectify the hazardous situation.

Not for the faint-hearted – having been built to ply American coastal waters, on the expedition to Murmansk Dasher *proved ill-equipped*

'It was well nigh impossible to obtain a foothold on the wet flight deck and although strenuous efforts were made to increase the tension on the restraining wires that remained, it became clear that it was a losing battle and decisions were soon made to assist the worst of the wildly moving Swordfish over the side.

'The order was then given for all personnel to leave the flight deck and we did not need to be told twice, in what was an atrocious situation and we left the unfortunate aircraft to their fate. Next morning, they had gone, leaving only a few tangled wires and other lashings as evidence that they had ever been there.

'If the flight deck was a hazardous place to be, the hangar was no better, except that it was shielded from the worst of the gale force winds and the driving snow squalls. In exactly the same way that the lashings had worked loose in the flight deck, so they replicated the procedure in the hangar. Aircraft began to tug at their lashings, which further loosened them and allowed Swordfish to career into Swordfish and Hurricane to career into Hurricane, with disastrous results.

HMS Dasher *pictured from the deck of the destroyer HMS* Blankney *while being escorted on her last fateful voyage to the Clyde estuary*

'The problem was then compounded by the loosening of ties and wires securing aircraft to the hangar roof, which ultimately fell on the aircraft moving around on the hangar floor. To add to this mêlée, the air fitters' and air mechanics' tool boxes broke loose from their stowage and commenced sliding from port to starboard, then back again. Eventually, like the flight deck, the hangar was declared out of bounds as it was a danger to life and limb.'

While all this was going on, in the torpedo room a torpedo had broken loose from its holding clamps and was creating havoc, rolling from port to starboard with each pitch of the ship.

One deck below the hangar, a member of the ship's crew recoiled in sheer horror as a huge split opened up on *Dasher's* side, just above the water-line. In complete astonishment he watched the convoy through the split on the ship's side, to a length of 60 feet, (18 metres) The American welding on the hastily converted aircraft carrier had come completely apart.

On reporting the damage to the captain, the duty officer was sent below deck to confirm the report from the crew member. When the duty officer confirmed the welding had come apart, the captain reported all the storm-related damage sustained to his ship to the convoy Commander, who immediately issued orders for *Dasher* to leave the convoy and seek shelter in Seydisfjorour, Iceland to wait out the storm before proceeding north/north west to Akureyri.

On entering Eyjafjorour, accompanied by two Royal Navy corvettes, *Dasher* slowly cruised past the small island of Hrisey which was situated in the middle of the fjord. As she did so, some of the ship's company and members of the Fleet Air Arm braved the freezing conditions and went out to the open deck, dressed in their Arctic clothing.

After the storm-damaged *Dasher* had been completely examined, she was classed as unfit for active service and it was decided that she should be escorted by the destroyer, HMS *Blankney* to Dundee where repairs would be carried out and the aircraft replaced.

On arrival at Dundee, *Dasher* entered the Caledon Shipyard for repairs. During her three weeks stay, Captain Boswell DSO took command of the aircraft carrier. Two of the crew who went home on shore leave were Frank Myers and Able Seaman William Vandyke. Both left on board all their personal belongings as they were due to rejoin the ship at Greenock, two weeks later.

Whilst in the shipyard, a fire occurred in the aircraft lift shaft between the hangar and the flight deck. The cause of the fire was recorded as: 'The over-loading of the lift and all the resistors in the electronics becoming red hot and igniting a discarded oil rag in the lift shaft.'

Whatever the cause, the repair work was completed and *Dasher* sailed for Rosyth. Within one hour of arrival, the ship was safely in dry dock. After a full examination of the ship's hull, all was found to be well and on the next tide, *Dasher* sailed for the Clyde via the Pentland Firth and the Minches. During the voyage the weather continued to be very bad and on reaching the sheltered waters of the Clyde estuary the crew of *Blankney* were quite envious to leave *Dasher* as their next journey was up through the storm-lashed Minches to Scapa Flow. Had the crew of *Blankney* known what was to befall *Dasher*, they would not have envied the crew their sheltered anchorage.

Dasher's safe arrival in the Clyde was the completion of another voyage unhindered by the enemy U-boats which remained unseen. On board the ship, the crew were in a relaxed mood. One of the engine room staff, Sub Lt Cameron telephoned home and told his sister, 'Tell mum she can sleep tonight.' These six words were a code between brother and sister which meant, 'We are in home waters.' In the family home everyone was relaxed knowing that Angus's ship was not in mid-Atlantic.

Due to the massive surveillance and sophisticated submarine detection stations in the area, Admiral Donitz, the officer in command of over 200 U-boats had issued an order to all his U-boat Kapitans, 'Under no circumstances was an attempt to be made to enter the Clyde estuary.'

On Friday 26th March 1943, *Dasher* sailed into Lamlash Bay, Isle of Arran and anchored overnight.

The ship's company mess deck a day before the catastrophe. All those in the mess deck were thought to have died instantly in the first explosion. Several relatives have identified their loved ones from this photograph

CHAPTER 9

SURVIVORS' ACCOUNTS

It is important for many reasons to know what had happened that brought life to a premature end for so many young men over fifty years ago. The *Dasher* disaster was just one sad chapter, perhaps, in a catalogue of catastrophes that, when added together, helped towards the greater goal of winning World War II.

Yet life is never so simple. Although trying to understand and examine the causes of the *Dasher* sinking has many benefits, historical, naval, logistical, none are of more worth than the opportunity that is offered to those caught up in the tragic events. Survivors and their families and friends, as well as bereaved relatives, even at this distance of time, have taken the opportunity to tell their stories.

On seeing the first editions of this book, many people have contacted us and have movingly told us their story. Because of the wartime conditions of secrecy in all matters that were in force in 1943, many have been telling their story and learning the stories of others for the first time. In this chapter and in the chapter of Precious Memories, those touched by the Dasher tragedy give their own report. The selection of stories are certainly gripping and we hope the experience of telling the tale has been of some belated comfort.

Captain AP Culmer DSC & BAR Royal Navy, Ship's Navigator

I had just moved down to my sea cabin to drink a cup of tea which my steward had got for me when it happened. I was lifting the cup to my lips when there was a terrific explosion and I was thrown across the cabin. Shaken but unhurt, I was up on the bridge within seconds just in time to see the complete 4.7 inch gun mounting from the stern sponson land in the sea about 70 yards (20 metres) away on the starboard side. Looking down the flight deck it was clear that the aircraft lift, weighing many tons, had been lifted off its mountings and hurled into the air. Aft of the lift well, the whole stern area was obscured by a large pall of smoke and dust.

The order Stop Engines was passed to the wheelhouse, although I doubt whether we had a propeller by then. On the bridge the two big escape ropes were released down to the water and with the ship having slowed from 15 knots to Stopped in the space of two or three minutes and the front end of the flight deck starting to lift as the after end sank lower, the pipe Abandon Ship went out.

With everybody else from the bridge gone, the Captain said to me, 'Away you go, Pilot. I'm just going to get my lifebelt.' As I was wearing a Vitabouy bridge coat I was able to give him my inflatable lifejacket which was on the chart table.

Climbing over the starboard side of the bridge, I started descending the rope hand over hand, but as I passed one of the openings at upper deck level somebody dived out and took me round the knees as though in a rugby tackle. I suppose it was a natural instinct that made me grip the rope more tightly to try and slow down our accelerated descent, but the only effect was to give me severe rope burns on both my hands, although I was not aware of these until many hours later. I then let go of the rope and my companion and I fell the last ten or twelve feet into the sea with those arms still locked tightly around my knees.

We seemed, my unknown and unbidden partner and I, to be going a long way down below the surface and it got darker and darker. Finally, scared we were going to continue our descent into the murky depths of the Clyde indefinitely, I managed to get the fingers of one hand round the neck of my passenger and with the fingers of the other jabbed for his eyes. Suddenly he released his morbid grip and thankfully I rocketed to the surface alongside a large float net on which was congregated a large number of officers but very few ratings.

As I arrived at the net the bows of the ship slid past with stern way on and her forefoot was already out of the water as she steadily sank by the stern. She assumed a completely vertical position for a few moments with only her bows sticking out of the water. Then they fell forward and she was gone. A deathly hush prevailed in sharp contrast to the bedlam of the preceding few minutes.

I now became aware that my neighbour on the net was Leading Seaman Dawson, my Chief Quartermaster. As we were exchanging news we noticed two men about fifty yards away and apparently in difficulties. As we were the only two on the net wearing any form of flotation equipment, we set off to swim over to them with the idea of bringing them back to the net for safety. As we arrived in their vicinity the sea started to effervesce, rather like a large tumbler of liver salts. At the same time we became aware of a very strong smell of petrol and then with a tremendous roar, the whole sea behind us suddenly burst into an inferno of flames.

Our position was precarious in the extreme as we were to leeward of the flames which were rising to a height of fifty or sixty feet (18 metres) and blowing in our direction. Fortunately we were clear of the burning petrol on the water and immediately set to swim as hard as possible for the north east corner of the fire and relative safety. After swimming hard for some time, towing our inert comrades, it became clear that the fire was gaining on us.

It was probably the hardest decision of my life to have to tell Dawson to let his man go and at the same time I let go of my own. It has haunted me on and off ever since, although I am convinced that had we persevered in our life-saving attempt, all four of us would have perished.

As it was, Dawson and I did manage to reach the safety of waters not threatened by fire and not long afterwards the *Isle of Sark*, the old Channel Islands ferry conscripted into naval service as a radar training ship, appeared and threw a rope to pull me alongside. Apparently, as eager hands were reaching down to pluck me aboard, the rope under my arms parted, the top of the ships's side struck me under the jaw and I fell all the way back into the sea unconscious. Thanks to two brave chaps who leapt in after me, I was soon roped again and hoisted on board like the proverbial sack of potatoes.

I remember nothing of leaving the rescue ship but recall vividly waking up in bed the next morning in a large airy room in the Kilmacolm Hydro Hotel which had been converted into a hospital. As consciousness returned all the pain seemed to be concentrated in my hands which I then realised were heavily bandaged. As my strength returned news of the casualties and survivors started to filter through. It seemed that those who left the ship over the port (ie windward) side, generally fared better because they were clear of the fire, the cause of most of the casualties.

The fire itself was due to aviation spirit floating to the surface several minutes after the ship had sunk and being ignited by a bit of burning debris or a calcium flare on a lifebelt. Apparently the main Avgas tank was still intact after the initial explosion because the No 2 Engineer, Lieutenant Seubert, who survived, was leaning against the after bulkhead of the engine room when it occurred. This was also the bulkhead of the Avgas tank.

The Captain, who also survived, had a very narrow escape from being pulled down to the bottom because of a broken wireless aerial wrapped around his neck. He was losing all hope when suddenly it slackened and my inflatable lifebelt shot him rapidly back to the surface. I don't think there were any survivors from the float net which Leading Seaman Dawson and I left on our ill-fated life-saving attempt. It must have been right near the heart of the fire.

The above report is extracted from an unpublished manuscript, Gold Lace written by Philip Culmer.

Able Seaman George T Lovegrove

After we had our tea, shore leave was piped for my watch but I was not keen on Greenock. My two shipmates, Bert Worsdell and Vicky Sporton tried their best to persuade me to go ashore with them but I declined. I was sitting in the mess deck chatting to some friends when there was a very loud bang which appeared to come from the stern of the ship. All the lights went out and there was a mad rush to the

George Lovegrove

stairway. I grabbed my packet of cigarettes off the table, stuffed them down the front of my belt and made my way aloft with the rest of my shipmates. On reaching the flight deck, I could see flames and smoke coming from the stern. I met up with two men whom I did not know and one of them asked me if I had heard the order to abandon ship. I replied that I had not.

Just then the ship began to list to starboard and I thought she was going to turn turtle. Suddenly she righted herself and began to go down quickly by the stern. I looked over the side and saw some men in the water. There was also a Carley raft. I did not jump there and then for fear of hitting someone in the water. Instead, I made my way to the port side of the ship which was by then, half-way under water. I then noticed that the aircraft lift was not elevated. Little did I know that it had been blown clear of the ship. *Dasher* was going down by the stern and by now the bow was about sixty feet (18metres) out of the water and I had great difficulty in standing upright. I looked towards the bridge but there did not appear to be anybody there. I then ran to starboard and jumped over the side, hitting the water feet first.

I thought that I was never going to surface. However on doing so I swam away from the ship as fast as possible as I did not want to be dragged under as she went down. When I was about 100 yards (30 metres) away, I turned round and was horrified to see her bows high in the water. I also saw three men on the bow and wondered why they had not jumped. One of them, standing with arms outstretched, shouted, 'Mum, I am a survivor.' I think he was off my own mess deck but I never saw him again.

Suddenly *Dasher* went under the waves with an awful grinding noise as everything movable slid back towards the stern. I saw a few men in the water, also a number of men on a Carley raft. I started to swim towards them when a great gush of black smoke came up from under the water. I felt the searing heat on my face and hands as I watched flames engulf the Carley raft. The cries and screams of those who were burnt to death in the water were terrible to hear. I swam away from the flames as

quickly as I could and it was then that I saw my shipmate, George Harkness from Kilmarnock and another called Ruggles. I tried to swim towards them calling out their names. However they drifted out of sight and another man came into view. He was in a very bad way, his hair had been burned off and his face was bloated. I grabbed him as he went by and he held on to me with a grip like a vice. I could not move my arms and we both went under. I managed to free myself from him but then he started to climb on top of me, trying to get out of the water. This time he pushed me right under and I was fighting for air. As I surfaced he made another grab at me but I evaded him and he slowly drifted away. Some time later a ship came straight towards me. I think it was a destroyer.

I then thought how lucky I was and I was going to be picked up. To my amazement the ship went straight past me. I saw men leaning over the port side but they did not attempt to throw a rope. I was so near to the ship, my hands were touching the side as she sailed past. I was trying to cling onto anything but the ship was so smooth there was nothing to get hold of. As I was fast running out of ship and I did not want to get mangled by the propellers, I turned over on my back, put my feet against the side of the ship and pushed myself away as hard as I could. As the ship sailed on, I was feeling quite exhausted and swallowed a lot of sea water. I began to think that I was never going to be saved.

To preserve my energy, I turned over on to my back, trying to float as much as I could. As I looked up at the sky I started to think about my family at home. I saw my widowed mother and my two brothers – they were going about their own routine not thinking that the youngest member of the family was fighting for his life. To try and conserve my strength I alternated between floating on my back and swimming the breast stroke. When I was on my back my heavy boots kept dragging me under. I had a sheath knife in my belt with which I tried to cut my boot laces, but each time I tried I went under. I gave it up as a bad job.

I do not know how long I was in the water but I was getting very cold and the sky was quite dark. By now I considered swimming ashore but I could not see any land. Out of the gloom another destroyer appeared. As it came alongside me they threw a rope which I held onto like grim death. They hauled me on board and as I hit the deck I passed out.

I woke up in a bunk with my feet and legs very cold. As I could not feel them I thought I had lost them. I then began to feel myself from top to toe and I just could not believe that I had not suffered any injuries. One of the crew came up and said, 'Thank goodness, we thought you were dead.'

On coming ashore at Ardross-an, I was taken to the local Royal Navy sick bay with other ship-mates, some of whom were very badly injured.

After attending the Royal Navy funeral I was put on a train with George and Charlie. We were bound for the Royal Navy barracks at Portsmouth. On departing from Ardrossan the railway guard was instructed to lock us in. I thought this was very stupid as the door was unlocked at Euston station from where we made our own way to Portsmouth barracks. On arrival at Portsmouth railway station we were suddenly surrounded by a Naval Police Patrol. We were bundled into the back of a Bedford truck and driven to an unmarked house in Southsea. At first we thought that we had done something wrong and that we would not be going home on leave after all.

One by one we were escorted into a room where three Naval officers sat at a large desk in a semi-darkened room. I was asked various questions concerning the sinking of *Dasher*, as were my two other companions. I can only think that they thought that we could throw some light on the disaster. Eventually we were dismissed and told to go on leave, much to our relief.

I have often wondered why I was saved when so many good men lost their lives. Perhaps if more had been wearing the regulation lifebelt many more would have been saved.

Tom Dawson

I was at the wheel of *Dasher* for the passage to Greenock and with me in the wheelhouse was Able Seaman Danny McCarthy. To us, the explosion was no more than a dull thud and seemed of little consequence until the bell on the fire alarm board began to ring and the various lights on the board indicated that fire had spread to many compartments below decks.

When after 30 seconds or so the deafening ringing of the bell ceased, we, enclosed as we were in the wheelhouse, were left in eerie silence, oblivious to the drama going on throughout the ship. I had been unable to contact the bridge and eventually it was the tilting of the deck that convinced us that we should evacuate.

Once in the water, I swam 50 feet (15 metres) clear of the ship and then turned to watch her dying moments. I saw the one remaining aircraft on deck break clear of its lashings and slither into the sea. I saw also, a man sitting on the extreme tip of the bow. I reflected that if the ship, on sinking, produced a suction, he would be the first to know. In the event, to my relief and no doubt to his, he was left floating on the surface. I then joined Danny who was clinging to a rolled up floatanet together with several others, one of whom, presumably remembering Coward's film *In Which We Serve*, began to sing *Roll Out the Barrel*. When none of us joined in the choir, he quickly dried up.

At that moment, the ship's navigator, who was supporting a man about 40 yards (12 metres) from us called for assistance. I swam over to him but it soon became obvious that the man was beyond help. Almost immediately, flames appeared on the surface and spread rapidly, emitting dense clouds of black smoke. I swam away as fast as I could but, having already spent twenty minutes or so in the very cold water, I was beginning to suffer from what we now know as hypothermia. At that time the word and its effects were not generally known.

My brain became dulled to the extent that I cared little whether I survived or not. Fortunately however, my arms and legs, almost on auto, continued to pump my gentle breast stroke. I made little headway but it kept me afloat. Eventually I was hauled onto a Carley raft and I promptly passed out. I came to some three hours later on board the *Isle of Sark*. A member of her crew was rubbing my legs and feet with a rough towel to promote circulation. He told me that he had been doing so for two and a half hours. He may well have saved my life.

When the final roll call was made, I was saddened to learn that Danny had not survived and that my girlfriend's brother, Able Seaman George Coulson, who would have become my brother-in-law, also perished.

Peter Leach

What happened to the 18 year old fireman who joined *Dasher* just three days before the disaster? Peter Leach relates,

On completing the fireman's course at the Fireman's Training School, London, I was posted to HMS *Mersey*, a land base, in Liverpool. On 23rd March I travelled to Greenock to join *Dasher*. On Saturday 27th, I was sitting in the mess deck, dressed to go on shore leave. I was talking to two greasers, one of whom gave me a tot of rum. After the terrible explosion, the place was a shambles, material was flying everywhere and all the lights went out. We managed to get to the middle deck without too much panic.

Charlie Weedon, who was an old merchant man said, 'Follow me.' When he jumped overboard, I remained on the ship. There was quite a number of us on deck when the ship gave a sudden lurch and we all fell over the side, the whole lot of us.

When in the water, I said goodbye to my mother, father, brothers and sisters. I must have blacked out for the next thing I remember was a Fleet Airman Sergeant pulling me onto a Carley raft which was packed with men. I noticed *Dasher* rise up by the bow and disappear. A plane was flying overhead and someone was signalling from the hills on land.

Just then the sea became ablaze and we were drifting towards the flames. Everyone left the raft, leaving me on my own. I had no option but to stay on board. The next I remember was a few lads on the *Isle of Sark* working on me with towels. They were trying to get me back to normal. It was not long before I was back on my feet and noticed a row of blankets covering the lads from the ship who had not survived. I pulled one of the blankets a little way back but I did not recognise him

We berthed at Ardrossan and when we left the *Isle of Sark* a captain shook our hands and wished us all he best. I had never met the captain of *Dasher* and I do not know if it was him or the captain of the *Isle of Sark*. It was a very sad ending to such a short stay on my first ship.

Robert Wanless

John Ferrier saved my life. How did it happen? I was just about to go down to the evaporator room, which was a compartment off the engine room, when John Ferrier, from Greenock, came into my cabin. John was telling me one of his latest jokes when the terrible explosion occurred. I was sitting on my bunk when the cabin blew in. The lights went out and I made my way along the passageway, under the flight deck. There were fires everywhere I went. At this point, the ship started to list to one side. It was a very serious list, so serious that I then decided to go back to my cabin, to get my lifebelt. As I reached my cabin the ship started to go down rapidly by the stern. I immediately about-turned and ran quickly to the foredeck which was sloping steeply by this time. Grabbing a hand rail, I pulled myself to the top of the slope, then jumped a great height from the blazing ship, into the sea. I had no lifebelt but there was a piece of heavy net in front of me and another sailor and I clung onto it.

Soon the netting was digging into my hands and the cold water was chilling me to the bone. We drifted towards a Carley raft, climbed aboard and settled down to await being rescued. No sooner had we settled when there was an almighty 'Whoosh' and flames rushed across the sea towards us. I immediately dived off the Carley raft and started swimming as fast as possible. I knew that I was swimming for my life.

After some time, I was picked up by a small boat and transferred to a Royal Navy ship. On coming ashore at Ardrossan harbour, I was taken to the Eglinton Hotel. I learned later that one of my shipmates had perished in the evaporator room, the very room where I had intended to go, when thankfully John Ferrier came to see me. His visit to me most probably saved my life.

Leading Signalman Edward Finch

Just after 4pm I left the flight deck and went to the mess deck for a game of cards. At 4.30pm it was announced over the tannoy that leave would be granted on arrival at Greenock. A few minutes later a messenger came down from the flag deck with a request from the other leading signalman who was on watch duty. He was requesting that I relieve him as he was going on leave when we docked at Greenock.

I threw in my cards and went to my locker to get dressed for duty. Just as I opened my locker door there was an almighty explosion and all the lights went out. My locker was near to an iron ladder which led three decks up. I was able to find the ladder in the darkness and joined many others in climbing to the upper deck. When we reached two decks up, it was obvious that we could not reach the third deck as the bulkheads were going, doors were jamming and *Dasher* was sinking fast. Some men, despite our warnings went back below deck to get their precious belongings and their lifebelts. We knew that it was too late for that but they would not listen. We never saw them again.

With only a minute or two to spare we started to slide down a rope which was dangling over the side. *Dasher's* bows were about 80 feet (24 metres) above the water. As I slithered down the rope, the man above me came down too fast and his boots struck me on the head. This caused me to lose my grip and I suffered rope burns trying to get hold again. By now, as the ship was sinking fast I let go of the rope and plunged into the sea. When I surfaced there was a lot of flotsam in the water, but I struck out away from the side of the ship, to get clear of the suction when she went down. After a while, I turned and trod water. Whilst I watched the ship, I saw a plane career down the flight deck and plummet into the sea, just before *Dasher* took her final plunge. After several minutes in the icy cold water, I reached a Carley raft with several men on it. Some other men were hanging on to it. With some others, I climbed aboard and the raft started to sink. At that precise moment, a huge bubble burst from the sea, where the ship had gone down. Petrol and oil spread out over the sea and all around us.

The petrol caught fire in the centre and rapidly spread. Just before it reached our raft, Telegraphist Allen and myself dived off and others left very quickly. I swam as fast and as long as I could under water. When I finally had to surface, there was nothing and nobody to be seen. It was terrible. There was fire everywhere. Fighting the cold, I swam gently around for about fifteen minutes before reaching a small coastal vessel. My fingers were frozen so I had to use the crook of my arms to climb the scramble nets onto the deck. The crew of the coaster were wonderful and in no time I was down in the engine room with a cup of hot drink in one hand, a cigarette in the other and a blanket draped over my shoulders. After thawing out, I went out on deck where there were two or three bodies. I was saddened to learn that Telegraphist Allen had not survived the terrible flames.

Able Seaman RWB Watts

We had just completed flying off and landing exercises. *Dasher* was proceeding upriver to Greenock and the ship's company had fallen out from Action Stations. I was in the bathroom getting cleaned up and the place was absolutely full. I had hardly stepped under the shower when all hell was let loose. There was this terrific explosion, the ship shuddered and darkness descended. I then experienced this very peculiar feeling. It was as if my body was being compressed. My eyes felt as if they were being forced up through my head. When I came around, all was on fire, no lights, just smoke, flames and debris. There was not a sound, a cry or any sign of another living person. I was praying and cursing all at the same time.

On this occasion, God let me off. Drowning did not enter my head. I was more concerned about being burned alive. After some more panic, something struck me on the head. Going down on my knees, under the flames and smoke, I noticed a dark patch. It was a doorway and it turned out to be my escape route from the bathroom. I suppose it is hard to understand a bathroom being on fire.

I made my way out into the Fleet Air Arm mess deck. There was no human sound, nothing but more fire and smoke. Everything was still in total darkness. It was then I noticed this violent swishing sound of water. I then glimpsed daylight just above the water line, starboard side of the ship. It was a gaping hole. I had a crazy notion for a second, of trying to escape through it. Something stopped me. I think it was the force of the swirling mass of water. Eventually I reached the deck above. I then tried to reach the hangar but it was an inferno. Minor explosions and aircraft ammunition were going off all around me.

Next, I made my way aft, to the torpedo flat. This was a working compartment. Here I made my first contact with living persons. Through the smoke I could make out a gathering around a bulkhead door. This was a means of escape to the upper deck but alas, the door was jammed tight. I shouted, 'Don't Panic.'

Then a miracle occurred, we managed to get the door open and surged through onto the deck. All this time, I was completely naked. The stern was well down in the water, the propellers were turning and the ship was still under way. I knew what I had to do. Some were already in the water. I had to join them. Someone yelled, 'Mind the bleeding screws.' (the propellers) I already had this in mind as I balanced on the port side of the ship and dived in. This must have been the longest dive ever. I reckon that I was swimming in the air before I hit the water.

In the sea, I never thought about drowning. Instead, I had this dread of a torpedo hitting me. To this day I still maintain that we were sunk by a torpedo. I overtook some chap in the water. He was fully clothed and wearing his lifebelt. I shouted to him, 'Remove your boots and swim as far away as possible from the ship.' I never knew whether he made it or not.

I kept on swimming, glancing back from time to time. Then it happened. *Dasher* slid under, stern first and bows high in the air. Just before she went under, sailors were still leaping from her. Minor explosions were still taking place, fire and smoke were everywhere. As the ship sunk the whole area of sea around us seemed to be on fire and I swam away from the flames as fast as I could. Eventually I was picked up by our own crash boat, ML528, transferred to a Royal Navy ship, landed ashore at Ardrossan and transported to Ballochmyle hospital. After a spell in hospital, I was transferred with another *Dasher* survivor from Kilmarnock, to a convalescent home which was on an estate, in Minnishant, a small village near Ballochmyle. I remember the River Doon ran through the estate.

Eric Hall

I was a member of the flying crew with the Fleet Air Arm Squadron on *Dasher* and not ship's company. We spent the day involved in take-off and landing practice. Flying trials had finished for the day and we were enroute for Greenock. Hands to Tea was piped over the tannoy. However as the menu consisted of Canadian Maple Syrup (treacle) which I have never liked, I did not go below for tea. My chum and I went to take some exercise on the flight deck when we heard on the tannoy that shore leave would commence on arrival at Greenock.

As we walked, there was an explosion aft and we saw the aircraft lift blown completely out and soar up in the air. Flames were coming from below in the hangar and the call went out for fire fighters. Just then, another explosion split the wooden flight deck lengthways. Immediately came the call, 'Abandon Ship.' Without any hesitation, I jumped off the flight deck into the sea. Although I was not wearing a lifebelt I managed to swim away from the ship. I just kept swimming. Unfortunately I swallowed some of *Dasher's* fuel oil. The sea water was black with oil. After some time, I was picked up and taken ashore at Ardrossan. As I had swallowed fuel oil, I was taken to hospital for treatment and one week later I was sent home on survivor's leave. I remember the day so vividly. No official reason has ever been given for the loss of *Dasher*. Perhaps it may never be.

Petty Officer Jeffrey Richard Gray

I placed my overall suit in a bucket of water to soak and then I decided to post a letter which had been in a pocket. Although in my underwear and barefoot I made my way via the cross passage to the Master of Arms office, to post the letter to my wife. Half way along the passage there was a muffled explosion and all the lights went out. What saved me was the flames from the hangar which lit up the passageway. I was thus able to ascend the port ladder into the hangar and out through the forward door onto the focastle.

I could see at a glance that something serious was wrong with *Dasher*. It was at such an angle that it was impossible to lower the lifeboat which we had released. Fortunately the lads recognised me as a Petty Officer. Although they were confused, there was no panic and they obeyed my order which was to release all Carley rafts. On the last raft going over the side, I said, 'All communication broken down, Abandon Ship.'

As *Dasher* sank by the stern, I jumped into the water, where a rating asked me what I intended doing. I did not know his name. I replied that being a swimmer I would make for the first raft that had been thrown over the side. It was by now the furthest from the ship. This would leave the nearest rafts for those who could not swim. The rating replied that he would accompany me. Enroute to the raft, we picked up an injured rating and conveyed him to the raft. I climbed aboard and he was handed up to me. He lay with his head on my lap. I pulled another rating onto the raft, whom I found out later to be Signalman Eddie Cane.

After *Dasher* sank, a coaster approached to pick up survivors. More by luck than by judgement, I was able to reach out and manoeuvre our raft round her bows and down her starboard. By which time her crew had lowered her lifeboat and we finished up between the coaster and the lifeboat. We then managed to climb on board the coaster, assisted by her crew.

Although as some might say I saved two lives, had we not got the Carley rafts away many more lives could have been lost. As for myself, I only did my duty, that which I had been trained for. We were taken to Ardrossan where we were met by the WVS who were marvellous. Seeing me in only my underwear, they supplied me with a pair of pyjamas, a pair of gym shoes and a gaudy sports jacket. What is more, they supplied us with a steaming hot mug of tea.

My admiration goes out to Lieutenant Commander Lane, our Royal Navy Executive Officer, who though fully clothed whilst in the water, swam from raft to raft and boosted the morale of the lads no end.

The following day he and I sat down and made out a nominal roll of survivors after

which those that could be fitted out were supplied with uniforms. He also supervised a casual payment for all so that we could inform our relatives that we were safe and that we would be home shortly. We were instructed not to mention what had happened to *Dasher*.

Three days later, I attended a court of enquiry which was held on board HMS *Archer* at Greenock. I was then drafted back to my home depot, HMS *Pembroke*, Chatham. From there I was sent on fourteen days survivor's leave, on completion of which, I was drafted into submarines, where I remained for the duration of the war.

E C Traill

I joined *Dasher* at Liverpool, just before Christmas 1942. I was only on the ship a few months and consequently I did not get to know many of the crew. On Saturday 27th March 1943, we were somewhere between Ardrossan and Lamlash, on voyage to Greenock. I had just strolled up to the afterdeck when the ship was hit or whatever, below the waterline. I thought it was going to collapse, but the inrush of water levelled it up.

I must have been leaning against the bulkhead because the vibration knocked me down and put a lump in the base of my spine which put my right leg out of action and I could not bear weight on it. We were so close to land that no one was wearing a lifebelt and there was no time to do anything about it as the ship sank within minutes. When I picked myself up, the water was washing the deck, about 20 feet (6 metres) above the waterline and by the time I had kicked off my shoes, boiler suit and sweater, the water was up to the rails. There must have been about sixty to seventy men on the deck by this time. All the rafts were lashed to the ship's side and could not be freed in time.

On jumping overboard I swam for fifteen minutes or so and was exhausted. I would definitely not have made it but one of our own deck planks appeared from nowhere. I was one of the ship's 'chippies' (joiners) and I recognised the plank to have come from the flight deck as I had made repairs to the deck many times. After holding on to the plank and floating for about fifteen minutes, our own crash boat, ML*528* picked me up.

I was at the area of the explosion and there was a distinct smell of explosives. A few mornings prior to the disaster, I heard on the radio news that there had been reports of enemy activity, saying that German planes had dropped mines in the area. In my opinion, the *Dasher* was either mined or torpedoed. I was not in attendance at the board of enquiry and no one asked me my opinion.

Able Seaman Frederick Nunn

Frederick was a Carlisle man and a gunner on the ship. He joined *Dasher* in Brooklyn. On disaster day he was in the mess deck, two decks down from the hangar, when the explosion took place.

Frederick immediately ran out to the passageway and climbed two ladders up to the hangar. As he was about to enter the hangar a large number of 'young boys' came cascading out screaming very loudly. Many of them had bad burns and flames were licking out of the hangar door. On looking into the hangar he could see the terrible flames from the explosion which had caused so much pain and death to the Fleet Air Arm personnel.

Realising that his escape route was not passable, he ran to the lifejacket store. They were stored in such a way that when one was removed, another rolled down and took its place. In this way they were easy to remove. Many of the crew did not try to make it to the lifejacket store as it was obvious that the ship was going down fast and the store was in an area that had been badly affected by the blast and the resulting flames.

Quickly taking another route, he came upon many of the watertight doors which were buckled and a number of the crew were trapped behind them. When Frederick reached the open deck, there was more calamity to follow as the Carley rafts could not be freed. The release clips would not budge and one of the sailors quickly produced a knife and cut through the holding ropes.

When a Carley raft was cast

into the water, he followed it by jumping overboard and clambering on. Within minutes the ship was gone and then came the flames. The sea was on fire and those on rafts paddled away from the flames, using their hands.

Whilst in the water, he swallowed a great deal of oil. After some time he was hauled from the Carley raft by the crew of the *Isle of Sark*. The crew took him below where they poured spoonfuls of rum down his throat.

The mixture of rum and oil made him feel very ill and he went up on deck where he was violently sick. This sickly feeling stayed with him for a long time, even when he was helped ashore.

The impression given on coming ashore was that the ship had hit a mine. Frederick was very upset when he was informed of some of the names of the missing. William (Barny) Barnes was one of the names. He was an Able Seaman with whom he had boxed, in many a fight, in New York. Another name was Sylvester Woollaghan, Sylvester, Barny and Fred were the best of friends.

After hostilities, Frederick joined the Shell tanker fleet and on one occasion his ship, the *Hallier*, visited Ardrossan, which had a Shell Oil Refinery. On coming ashore, Fred visited the lounge of a hotel and started chatting to a local. When he mentioned *Dasher*, the local informed him that there were some graves of *Dasher* boys in Ardrossan cemetery. Fred visited the cemetery and was dismayed to learn that another friend, 'Pincher' Martin was buried there. Fred had never been told of the number of fatalities nor had he made contact with another survivor.

Ordinary Seaman Michael Albert Dury

Michael has never been able to erase the memory of the disaster. He was one of the ratings who were trapped behind a jammed watertight door which was released and held open by Petty officer John A Stamp. At the board of enquiry he brought John Stamp's bravery to the attention of all.

Robert Babington DSC, QC

As a young Sub Lieutenant Robert Babington was the Observer flying in a Swordfish aircraft which landed on *Dasher*. He relates,

We landed on *Dasher* on the afternoon of Saturday 27 March 1943. The ship was situated in the Clyde and when I saw her before the explosion was heading towards the Isle of Arran. The weather was fine and good. After we landed my pilot and myself got out of the aircraft and went into the Commander Flying Officer's office situated on the 'Island' on the Starboard side of the ship. We were in the process of reporting to him when the explosion occurred. Almost immediately the ship lurched and went down astern, rather more on the port side.

I went out of the office and back on the flight deck when the ship began to settle quite slowly by the stern. I don't remember seeing anyone else although there must have been some. I crossed the flight deck to port side and went onto the walkway just below the flight deck on the port side. I remember as I stood there something very large hurtled down the deck and into the sea at the stern; this was because of the ever-increasing inclination of the flight deck. I looked to my left as I was standing on the walkway and found that I could see far below in the entrails of the ship a large fire raging. Again I don't remember seeing any other people near me at this stage.

It was obvious to me the ship was sinking. I was clothed in a flying suit and Mae West. I jumped feet first into the sea and struck out vigorously away from the sinking ship. I had heard that when a large ship went down one should get, as far away as possible otherwise one would be sucked down with it. I was very glad to have my Mae West on but it does hamper speed through the water. I looked back towards the ship and by this time she was practically vertical in the water, the bow pointing towards the sky. Inside I could hear awful bangs, explosions and screams. She slowly slid down and disappeared. At this time I began to notice other men in the water and some Carley Floats with some people in and near them. I swam towards a float – it was

quite near but I decided to leave it to others as I had on my Mae West. I remember seeing one man with his head split open. Just then there was a boiling sound in the water and flames shot high in the air as the surface of the sea caught fire. I turned and swam away from the flames. I escaped from the fire but a number of men were caught and burned to death. I was fortunate in that the wind was blowing the flames away from me.

The next thing I remember was a ship arriving. It had put down scrambling nets and a rope ladder; I went up the rope ladder, to be met on deck by a number of young Indian ratings of the Royal Indian Navy. They supplied me with tea and dried my clothes. I cannot remember the name of this ship.

I can remember nothing else until I arrived in Belfast enroute to Dublin where my parents then lived. While in Belfast I went to see my cousin, Lord Justice Babington who was just about to go to assize. He insisted that I go with him and got a taste of a very different sort of life in which later I was able to enjoy myself.

I have always believed my aircraft was the last to land because of the short time interval between our landing and the sound of the explosion in the Flying Officer's office. Also I remember no other aircrew entering or going towards the office.

One thing leads to another and it seems to me that anyone interested in the *Dasher* tragedy enough to read what I have written so far would also be interested in the ship's earlier history as known to me. I joined HMS *Dasher* some months before her sinking as an Observer in a Firefly squadron. At the time I joined her she was in Scapa Flow. So far as I can recollect her role was to provide air cover for convoys going to Russia and also for whatever ships of the navy might be at sea. Particularly I remember being told of the importance of shooting down the big German Reconnaissance aircraft, which the Germans used to shadow the convoys and transmit their positions to U boats.

In one operation that I am aware of that *Dasher* took part in she left Scapa Flow with some escorts and headed north. I don't remember seeing any of the large ships but the weather was very bad and visibility was very poor. Nevertheless we had two air crew and two planes ready to take off at all times. We ploughed on in a northerly direction whilst the weather grew steadily worse. The ship seemed to make heavy weather of the very formidable sea, and I remember on one occasion when I was on deck she seemed to get across the wind which caused her to list right over and suggested to me she might turn turtle. The creaks and groans of the structure of the ship were awful to listen to. Flying in those conditions was impossible but we still kept our state of readiness. It was not possible to

stand on the flight deck. I remember being told by someone that the anenometer had jammed at a recorded wind speed of 120 knots. Quite suddenly all was quiet. I remember waking up one morning and everything was still. I went on deck and found that the ship had gone into a fjord and anchored in Iceland. I learned that the captain had decided to repair some of the storm damage in the quiet sheltered waters. The scenery was wonderful with no sign of life whatsoever. The ship was careened over on her side and welders went down and repaired a large split that had opened there. After the patching-up had been completed we sailed straight back to the Clyde. I remember the journey through the Minches when the sea was quite calm, a great change from what it had been a few days before.

Ordinary Telegraphist Fred Plank

It was Saturday 27 March 1943. I was just 19 years of age with two months to go to my 20th birthday. HMS *Dasher* was my first ship; I had joined her at Greenock in October 1942, just in time to sail to Oran, North Africa.

Captain Boswell had announced over the loudspeaker system that leave was being granted on arrival at Greenock This was followed by an announcement regarding pay parade. I was standing in the mess, wondering if I had time for a shower before the pay parade when there was a loud bang and we were plunged into darkness. The ship rolled over a very long way to starboard, eventually stopped and slowly righted itself. It was very quiet apart from a few metal bangs as men grabbed things from their lockers. I thought it best to go on deck and followed an orderly queue up the companionway.

'What's happened? What's happened?' was the question everyone was asking. 'I don't know but I am going to my Abandon Ship Station' was the common reply. That is what most of us did calmly. On the way I met Jock Jenkins, another Telegraphist, who had just been in the shower and was clad only in a towel. He was muttering, 'I will catch my death.' (I met him ashore later; apart from some minor injury he was OK.)

I made my way up to my Abandon Ship Station, a Carley Float on the Port side. A group of men were trying to lower a raft but the main rope had jammed. They were shouting for a knife to cut the rope. At that moment Captain Boswell came across the flight deck. 'Don't let them go,' he said, 'she's still afloat!' I thought, 'What is he talking about – still afloat?' As I looked around I could see the stern going down, all around men were jumping into the water. As we had aerial wires stretched between the gun platforms along each side of the ship I jumped over as far as possible, I did not want to get tangled on the aerial

Fred Plank

wires. I was wearing trousers, a jumper and deck shoes. It did not occur to me to kick off my shoes.

The day had been bright and sunny with a lively breeze and I thought, 'It should not be too bad.' When I hit the water all the breath was knocked out of me with the cold. I kept going down a long, long way until I decided that I had to get to the surface. I kicked out and started to rise. As I approached the surface I kept hitting my head on what felt like pieces of wood, fortunately I did not receive any injuries.

I was swimming towards a raft when I came upon one of our stokers that I knew by sight. He had hurt his arm and was floundering about in some difficulty. I managed to calm him and help him over to a float-a-net. I told him to hang on whilst I tried to reach a Carley float. An empty raft passed near me but it was moving so fast there was no chance of me getting onto it. An empty 50-gallon drum floated nearby and I was able to hang on.

There were several men near me; our eyes were glued to the bow triangle until the shout went up, 'She's going.' We watched as the ship slipped beneath the waves. We all feared for the undertow but strangely it didn't happen. There I was clinging to the oil drum wondering what to do, when suddenly a terrific fire spread across the sea, there were masses of flame leaping high in the air until they were hidden in a cloud of smoke. My oil drum lost its attraction and I swam away from it as fast as I could. It was then I discovered that you couldn't see very far when you are swimming in the sea, even when the waves are fairly light. There was just me, the sea and the sky. I was frightened and I felt so alone.

I swam on and came across a piece of wood about 12 feet long (3 metres) it was a relief to hang onto it. As I floundered about I spotted Bob Powell and a Fleet Air Arm chap, I knew both, as they were Telegraphists. As the fire around us became more and more intense we realised we were being carried towards it. We all desperately kicked out, trying to get away from the intense heat from the flames. Fortunately the smoke was being blown away from us.

At last we spotted a mast and soon a ship was coming towards us. I swam towards it until I made out the identification number on the ship's side, it was U 92. My thoughts were of camouflaged U boats. Then I thought this was being ridiculous. They were in the process of lowering a boat and I was relieved to hear unmistakable English voices. When the boat hit the water I waved and yelled to attract their attention. They rowed towards me and heaved me aboard.

I thanked them profusely and when I asked if I could take an oar the Coxswain agreed. This helped to warm me up and I was glad to be occupied in doing something useful. We picked up more survivors and returned to the ship where willing hands helped us up the scrambling net to a warm welcome.

U92 was in fact a French sloop, the *La Capricieuse*, but manned by a British crew. I was taken below where the crew were working hard trying to revive four or five men laid out on the mess tables. I don't know if they were successful. The ship had picked up 26 survivors but unfortunately seven died before reaching Ardrossan. I was asked to identify some oil-soaked bodies but I was unable to recognise any of them. It was not a pretty sight.

One of the cooks gave me his overalls, they were a bit tight under the armpits but I was grateful for the dry clothing.

La Capricieuse was the first rescue ship to arrive at Ardrossan Harbour. It was still daylight. There were emotional farewells to our rescuers as we went ashore. The injured were helped into waiting ambulances and taken to the local naval sick bay.

We were taken to a disused school where we received a warm welcome from Wrens and Women's Voluntary Service Ladies. (WVS)

There was disbelief and deep shock as we began to discover the extent of the tragedy.

We got a bit of light relief when the WVS kitted us out with emergency clothing. They did a wonderful job, although some items were a bit exotic, one chap was strutting about in plus fours. They could not improve on my overalls so I had to continue wearing them. After a meal and some beer we tried to settle down for the night with the offer of two aspirins. Needless to say, there wasn't much sleep for anybody.

Sunday was a dull, dank, miserable day with thick mist. I recall thinking how much worse it would have been if the weather had been similar on the Saturday. We were confined within the school with nothing to do except to relate our particular experiences and enquire about our shipmates. We made statements to a preliminary enquiry and we went in small groups, to HMS *Fortitude* (the Naval Base in Ardrossan) to see if we could identify any of the bodies there. By the time my group got there in the afternoon there were only two who hadn't been recognised.

We heard that some charred life rafts and other flotsam had been brought ashore. During the next three days we were issued with such uniform as the base could provide. We were also given an advance of pay. This boosted morale considerably and we began to feel much more like sailors and less like castaways.

The funeral was arranged for Wednesday and, at last, we were allowed out of the naval base on Tuesday night. Of course most of the lads went off to the pub and, although some of the lads drank too much, the local people and police were very sympathetic. Bob Powell and I enjoyed the famous Scottish hospitality at the home of one of the Wrens, a pub in Kilwinning.

On Wednesday afternoon we formed up for the funeral, there was a Royal Marine band playing the doleful Dead March followed by two draped lorries carrying the coffins, then the survivors with me in the front rank. We slow-marched through the town to the cemetery. On the way we passed a school with flag at half-mast and all the pupils formed up in a silent tribute. That affected me deeply. We lined up around the graves and I was detailed to help lower a coffin. As soon as the ceremony was over the band struck up Colonel Bogey and we marched off back to the school. So life goes on.

'Hurry up and get your tea, you are on draft,' was the greeting. Soon we set off for the train to Glasgow, where we caught the night train to London, a very long journey in wartime, and then on to Chatham. We reached the barracks about mid-day where the Bosun welcomed us with 'Survivors eh! I'll soon have you bastards out of here.' He summoned several of his slaves (messengers) with orders to take us through the joining routine and see that we got absolute priority throughout. (This procedure could take up to three days, more if you wanted to stretch it out as there were long queues at the many offices that had to be visited.)

I left on two weeks survivor's leave about 1730 hours and went straight home to a highly emotional reunion with my family. They had realised that something dramatic had happened when I wrote from Ardrossan saying I hoped to see them soon. I went to bed early and slept soundly until the evening of the next day. I really don't remember much about that leave but my sister told me that I could not stop talking.

Leading Seaman George Powell

George was drafted to the USA when the merchant ship was being converted and knew every part of the ship. He reports,

I was at the stern with a group of about twelve others. Suddenly there was a blinding sheet of flame and a terrible explosion. The next thing I knew I was lying on my back looking at the sky with the most agonizing pain in my back and head.

I could feel a hand touching mine; it was Arthur Clark's hand.

All of the others were dead.

Arthur and I made for the ladder to reach the flight deck. The hanger looked like Dante's inferno. There were flames everywhere and a great deal of smoke. We could hear terrible screams everywhere. The boxes of ammunition beside us were now on fire, the heat was awful and the bullets were firing away. The noise of the firing bullets clattering against the ship was frightening. The warheads on the torpedoes stored beside the ladder were almost red hot from the flames around them.

When we reached the side of the ship I told Arthur I was not a good swimmer. Just before he dived in Arthur told me to jump after him and he would support me. I stepped over the chains and did a shallow dive. The impact of the sea was like hitting solid concrete. On reaching the surface Arthur was gone.

On deciding to remove my shoes I tried to lift my foot to untie the lace but each time I bent down my head went under the water, so that idea was abandoned.

As the ship sank by the stern my last look at her as she slipped beneath the waves was to see the flight deck and the 20mm gun positions, the bow and the two 4inch guns pointing to the sky.

The screams and curses will live with me forever, the sight of those lads clinging to the gun positions, screaming. Some of them on jumping off were dropping on the heads of those in the sea beneath them. The bow was now pointing to the sky. *Dasher* sank slowly, gathered speed then she was gone.

I was very frightened. I looked around for something to cling to but was nothing I could see. I called to God then to my mother. Having started to scream I could not stop, I screamed and screamed. Around me was the smell of petrol that had surfaced from the broken tanks of high octane for the aircraft. Suddenly the petrol ignited. I tried to swim around the flames but I was trapped, no matter which way I went the flames surrounded me. It was terribly hot. I tried to splash the flames but that had no effect. My hair caught fire and I dipped beneath the water but on surfacing my hair caught fire again within seconds. I thought that if I had to die I would rather drown than be burned to death. I dived under the water, taking a big mouthful of water, and I also breathed water up my nose as I was sinking.

I started to go down in a sitting position; the water was a lovely pale green. I was still going down, breathing in water to get it over with quickly. The shade of green darkened until it was a deep bottle green colour. Around me the brightest of lights flashed about, and then I felt nothing but peace, no more swimming, no more flames and heat. No more screaming, no more screams of my pals, just quiet, beautifully quiet and I was so sleepy. I knew that once I fell

sleep I was gone but I wanted it so badly.

I was almost gone when I heard a voice, a loud distinct voice saying, 'Get out of this and you will go home on leave.' I was awake, and swam upwards. No more taking in water, I was getting up fast. On reaching the surface the flames and smoke were behind me. A motor torpedo boat was approaching and a rope was thrown but I was so exhausted I could not get a firm grip. A crew member jumped into the water and put the rope around me. On being pulled to the side of the boat I was hauled out of the water.

On reaching the port of Ardrossan I was ushered with ten other wounded survivors into a waiting ambulance and taken to the Royal Navy Sick Bay in the town. When our clothes were cut off we realised that we were all black, from head to toe from the ship's diesel oil. During our stay in the Sick Bay the screams from the badly burned were horrendous. One lad who had been blown out of the side of the ship had received such terrible burns all over his body.

The following day I was taken with others to the mortuary to identify the bodies. Some were so badly burned they could only be identified by rings on fingers or tattoos.

After attending the funeral I was given two weeks survivor's leave.

The Dasher Man Who Was Lucky Twice Able Seaman Bernard John Anderson

I was married on 3rd September 1939, as we left the church and stood for photographs, people were running past shouting out, 'War has been declared.' A fine start to married life.

I joined the Royal Navy and was based at Chatham where I met Wilfred Ferneyhough. We became very firm friends and were glad that both of us were posted to join HMS *Dasher* over in New York. With a party of others we sailed on board the troopship *Queen Mary* bound for Canada. After a very fast journey across the Atlantic we arrived in Canada where we boarded trains bound for New York. We continued our journey stopping at a place called Truro where it was drawn to our attention that some lads had deserted the train.

While in New York I was posted to US Navy Barracks Staccato, Brooklyn where I was involved in armed sentry sabotage watch. I can remember collecting navy personnel wages armed with a revolver in public and was instructed not to be afraid to use it. I was accompanying a chief petty officer with a chauffer.

The converted aircraft carrier HMS *Dasher* was about to commence sea trials when we went on board. During the next few days a number of problems were experienced with the ship's engine. One explosion in the engine room caused the ship to return to dock for further repairs. While waiting for *Dasher* to be repaired at the US Navy dockyard at New York HMS *Penelope* docked on 19th May for extensive repairs. She had been severely damaged by enemy aircraft at Malta and was riddled with holes. The lads re-named her HMS *Pepperpot*.

When the first of four aircraft attempted to land on *Dasher*, one plane went over the side; fortunately the pilot was unharmed apart from a soaking. Another plane crash-landed onto the flight deck and all this was just in the first few days.

I enjoyed my time in New York and tried to see as many musical shows as possible. We were given passes to see *Porgy and Bess*. I loved to sing and entertain the lads. I missed my big moment when I was invited to sing on *Captain Bill's Half Hour* but had to sail on *Dasher* before my debut.

I was happy on *Dasher* and got on very well with many of the officers. Whilst home on leave I became ill and was confined to bed. The family doctor arrived and diagnosed appendicitis. After being operated on at the local hospital I became very seriously ill with peritonitis. As I was not expected to survive the parish priest was summoned to my hospital bed where the last rites were performed.

I was still on sick leave when I heard the terrible news that HMS *Dasher* had sunk. My close friend Wilfred Fernyhaugh was posted missing presumed dead.

I really had two lucky escapes as I survived after receiving the last rites and whilst I was recovering from my illness I missed being back on board the ill-fated *Dasher* when she exploded.

Lt David McNair

When army officer Lieutenant David McNair was granted leave he usually headed for the Island of Arran to spend time there with his many friends at the village of Corrie. On Friday 26 March 1943 he was out and about walking with some of his chums. As darkness fell they were making their way back to Corrie when they heard the steady drone of overhead planes. They were not familiar with the engine noise and decided the aircraft were German. It was hoped the planes were not on a mission to drop mines in the busy shipping channel between Arran and the mainland.

The next morning Lieutenant McNair was due to catch the ferry back to Ardrossan. Unfortunately he missed the bus back to Brodick where the ferry was docked and had to borrow a bicycle. A telephone call was made to the harbour master at Brodick pier advising him that an army officer would be arriving a few minutes after the departure time. The ferry captain agreed to wait while the young lieutenant speedily cycled round the bay anxiously keeping his eyes on the waiting ferry. Once Lieutenant McNair was safely on board the ship departed. The army officer made his way to the open top deck and during the voyage to Ardrossan he noticed a small aircraft carrier sailing behind the ferry.

When the ferry was approximately half way into her voyage Lieutenant McNair heard a loud blast out to sea. He saw in the distance a pall of black smoke and flames. The aircraft carrier had exploded. The Lieutenant immediately thought, 'That could have been us!' He wondered if there had been any connection with the planes the previous evening.

The ferry did not slow down or alter course but continued towards the mainland. On entering Ardrossan Harbour (HMS *Fortitude*) all the passengers were ushered downstairs to the lounge. When they were all seated two gentlemen in civilian clothes addressed them. They introduced themselves as 'Security' and proceeded to instruct all the passengers that they must not speak about the incident.

The lieutenant put the incident from his mind and returned to duty. He heard no more about it and as instructed, he never ever spoke of it. During his wartime service he was attached to 463 Squadron Royal Canadian Air Force and saw service in Burma, India and Indonesia, where he attained the rank of captain

At the end of his army career in 1946 he decided to take up a career in education. Many years later he retired as Dean of Education at Manchester University.

Fifty three years later the ex-army captain returned to the Isle of Arran to enjoy a holiday with his wife. During his visit he mentioned to a group of locals that he had visited the island during wartime. When he mentioned the explosion, the smoke and flames he was told that a book had been published about the incident. For the first time David McNair found out the ship involved was HMS *Dasher*.

Some young men survived the Dasher tragedy by sheer good fortune. They should have been on the ship on the fateful afternoon but events intervened, thus saving their lives.

Roy Williams

Roy was a member of the Fleet Air Arm on board *Dasher*. He was home on leave in Lancashire. On 23rd March, he was at a dance and he met a young girl. They enjoyed each other's company so much that they arranged to meet the following evening for a date. The next day he received a telegram instructing him to report back on board *Dasher* on 26th March.

As he had no way of communicating with his new girlfriend, he decided that as he did not want to lose touch with her, instead of returning to his ship immediately, he would wait and meet her as planned to explain that he had to leave there and then to catch the train to Scotland. After meeting her that evening, he travelled to Greenock to join *Dasher*. When he arrived, on Friday 26th March 1942, he was informed that the ship had just sailed. For the next two days, Roy tried to join the ship as he was informed that it was 'On exercise duties in the Clyde estuary.'

On his second evening at Greenock, Roy was devastated to be told that *Dasher* had blown-up. He had lost a great deal of good friends and his ship, but he was very thankful that the delay in travelling to meet and explain the situation to his new found girl, had probably saved his life.

He was handed a rail warrant and two weeks survivor's leave, because 'it was in the books that he was on the ship.' On arrival home he made a point of meeting his girlfriend and he told her that *Dasher* had been torpedoed. He never mentioned the ship again. In October 1946 they were married. During their happy married life, Roy always liked to mention the fact that his wife Dora had saved his life. After forty nine happy years together, Roy passed away in October 1995.

John Jeffrey Wallis

John Wallis, a Naval rating from Aberaeroin, Dyfed, was 18 years of age when he completed his training at Chatham barracks. He was due to go on 72 hours leave when Jack Barratt, one of his friends, who was attached to the Drafting Office, informed him that a draft had come through for him. The draft instructions were to the effect that he was posted to HMS *Dasher* and he was to join the ship at Greenock. On enquiring about rail passes his friend told him to proceed immediately on his 72 hours leave and report to him on his return. He did as he was told and with another rating they were issued with rail passes to Greenock.

After a long tedious journey they eventually arrived at Greenock and reported to the Drafting Master at Arms, who to their surprise, greeted them with the words, 'You lucky pair of b---s, come and have a drink with me.' It was most unusual for a rating to socialise with a Master of Arms. However on seeing the look on their faces he advised them that, '*Dasher* has gone down with terrible loss of life. You had best return to Chatham barracks. On arrival back at Chatham they were told, 'It sure was a close thing.'

John Wilson

John Wilson from Henleaze, Bristol was a member of 816 Squadron, Fleet Air Arm on board *Dasher*. His best friend was Leading Writer William Gillies. When on shore leave, they spent a great deal of time walking on the hills together. Towards the end of March 1943, William was on duty and John had been working ashore for a few days. On his arrival back at Greenock on March 27th, to rejoin *Dasher*, he was informed that the ship had been lost with a very high loss of life. He learned later that his friend, William was not one of the survivors. Another friend on board, Sandy Thomson was listed as missing. Sandy was a Naval Airman. John had lost a lot of good friends and of course all his personal belongings. It was 51 years later that he was informed by John Steele that his friend William had been buried in Greenock Cemetery.

Rev Frank Myers, Telegraphist

It was with mixed feelings that my name appeared on the draft list in Chatham barracks for *Dasher*. *Dasher* was in Brooklyn Navy Yard in New York and we were to be part of the initial commissioning party. Arrival in New York brought us a heat wave and having to cope with kitbags and hammocks while still dressed in winter uniform. We were in Brooklyn navy barracks which, compared with Chatham, was out of this world, not only in standards but in food. Also because the ship was not ready we had New York before us. All the theatres and concerts were available free, from the Carnegie Hall to the Radio City Music Hall, from the cinemas to the shows featuring such as Tommy

Roy Williams (above) owed his life to his meeting with his future wife Dora

Dorsey's band. We almost felt guilty enjoying such unrationed and unrestricted lighting conditions, while Britain was suffering utility hardship and darkness.

The time came for working on the ship. What a change from my previous ship, the *Woolston*, a 1917 destroyer – so cramped but obviously dedicated to a warlike purpose. Here was the original merchant superstructure and bridge and large capacity holds with a flight deck superimposed. She had been laid down as a banana boat, the *Rio de Janeiro*.

The journey to the United Kingdom was uneventful, although there were signs of what was to be our lot. She rolled to great extent. There was a feeling of insecurity, but it was our lot to be on the ship and

nothing could change it. An operation to the North African landings brought a satisfaction of doing something worthwhile, but after the landings were consolidated, we were no longer required.

Our next operation was to take part in the Russian convoys. The sea was so rough on our way to Iceland that the *Dasher* was badly damaged. There were not a few who were disturbed by the ship's motion. One kept away from the flight deck for to see its slope made it seem impossible to keep any foothold. One officer spent most of the time on the lee of the ship out on deck for fear that she would capsize.

Because of the damage we were ordered back to Dundee for repair. It was in Dundee, just days before departure to the Clyde and disaster, that I left the ship. One looks back on the appalling loss of life on *Dasher*. Many of my friends were lost there and the tales which were recounted as I met up with the survivors were horrendous – aviation spirit ignited on the water and some men were burned alive.

One might imagine my mixed feelings as I was eventually drafted whilst in the Pacific to a similar ship. Was it to be the same story again? The answer was soon found for lessons had been learned. The *Striker* was a far more stable ship and had many things that *Dasher* didn't, and indeed was a much happier ship to be on. The feeling was that the first four ships, *Archer*, *Avenger*, *Biter* and *Dasher* were adapted too quickly without much thought behind them.

After becoming a minister in Springburn, Glasgow, I conducted two funerals, one soon after the other. One was for a woman who had not got over the death of her favourite nephew in 1943. He left home in the morning and never came back. He was on *Dasher*. Soon after at the second funeral I was introduced to the widow's sister, whose husband was killed on *Dasher*. He was a seaman who did hairdressing on his off-watch time and had many times cut my

hair. This experience compelled me to go to Ardrossan to look at the graves of the bodies recovered (so few). One was someone I should have known but didn't and could only come to the conclusion that he was my relief.

William Vandyke

William, an Able Seaman from London, joined *Dasher* in America as a member of the Care Maintenance Party and was on board when the ship was commissioned on July 1, 1942 at Brooklyn, New York. He remained with the ship throughout Operation Torch and the terrible voyage to Murmansk, when they were diverted because of severe storm damage to North East Iceland.

After temporary repairs were carried out, *Dasher* sailed to Dundee. It was when the ship was berthed at Dundee that William left on March 1, 1943, to attend a course. On the very same day that William left *Dasher*, Captain Lentaignes and another member of the crew also left the ship. The other crew member had been a writer with *Punch* magazine. His name was Brocklebank.

When William learned about the fate of *Dasher*, he never ever believed that the ship blew-up. His thoughts were that it was either a torpedo or a mine.

Some people witnessed the disaster from the Isle of Arran.

Alister McKelvie, Seaview Farm, Brodick

Saturday 27th March 1943 was my eleventh birthday. I was walking through a field to help my parents plant potatoes. My father shouted at me, 'Something dreadful has happened to that aircraft carrier.'

We did not have a very good view of what was happening but we could see a tremendous amount of black smoke and there was a plane flying over the area. I ran over to our neighbours as I knew that from there, I would have a better view. On reaching the house, the two brothers, Dougie and Archie Cook were standing outside. Dougie said to me, 'It's a terrible tragedy. The water's on fire!'

Dougie had been looking through the binoculars and he handed them to me. I could then see a wall of flame about twenty feet high and colossal black smoke. I could also see some activity at Brodick pier and I made my way down to it.

On reaching the pier *The Two Boys*, a naval vessel not unlike a fishing boat, was on its way out to the disaster area. I waited about the pier until *The Two Boys* returned. There were no survivors or fatalities aboard and the navy grey paint on the vessel was all blistered with the heat from the burning sea.

Over the next day or two I made enquiries at Lamlash pier and I was told that like Brodick, no survivors or bodies were recovered by the boats that had departed from Lamlash.

As there were no reports in the newspapers about the sea tragedy, due to censorship, I always thought that everyone aboard the aircraft carrier had perished. Due to the very sad circumstances I will never forget my eleventh birthday.

Reg Summerscales, Old Blairbeg, Lamlash

During 1942/43 I was stationed at the Signal Squadron, Kings Cross Point on the Isle of Arran as a signalman, Royal Navy. There was during my period there a lot of 'working up' of new ships. Among them were aircraft carriers which were always heavily involved in deck landing training with their aircraft.

I was on duty on Saturday 27th March 1943. At 09.00 I watched *Dasher* as she sailed from Lamlash Bay, Isle of Arran to carry out deck landing training. I observed her in the Clyde estuary during the day. At 16.30 *Dasher* called us by the lamp. The signal which I received read –

TO FLAG OFFICER IN COMMAND, GREENOCK

FROM HMS *Dasher*

ESTIMATED TIME OF ARRIVAL, TAIL OF BANK, GREENOCK 18.00 HOURS

The signal was telephoned to

Naval Officer in Command (NOIC), Lamlash for onward teleprinter transmission to Greenock. On leaving the phone I looked out and

noticed some smoke coming from *Dasher* astern below the flight deck and I informed Naval Officer in Command, Lamlash. At first I thought that an aircraft had crashed but she had recovered all her aircraft. I tried to contact *Dasher* by lamp but I received no reply. Soon after she disappeared stern first, amid smoke.

I was ordered to Keep the *Dasher* Incident Quiet and Never Repeat Anything Which I Had Witnessed.

Little did I know in 1943 that the loss of life would be so great and it was not until 1991 that I ascertained the very high number who had perished.

William John McCrae, Artificer Sergeant Major

I was born on the island of Arran and as a teenager I decided to make a career for myself in HM Forces. Although many years have passed, I still remember very vividly one particular Saturday afternoon on the island. I was gathering firewood and I was being helped by my brother, Duncan and a friend, Jimmy Campbell. Jimmy and his family were evacuees from war torn Glasgow.

As the three of us emerged from a wood, which was halfway between Corrie and Sannox, we noticed smoke out to sea. It was very black smoke. I could make out the outline of a ship which was going up at the bow and the

sailors were jumping overboard.

We were in a direct line from the ship and it was a very clear day. Everything that was happening seemed to be so close to us. As we were looking at the burning ship, there were planes flying overhead.

As we stood watching, the ship started to go down at the stern. Just then Mr Laughlin Milne, a local artist came over to us and hurried us away from our vantage point. His intentions were kind as he was trying to spare us possible unpleasant scenes. He said to us that it was probably an exercise.

I made enquiries on the island about the incident. However nobody seemed to want to discuss the subject. It was not until 1993 when a plaque was being unveiled in Ardrossan that I became aware of the large loss of life from the sea disaster that I had witnessed with my brother and Jimmy Campbell.

Mrs Elizabeth Schlund, Lochranza

In 1943 I was a coding officer in the WRNS attached to Cypher Communication, Greenock. On Saturday 27th March 1943 I was on leave in Arran and cycling along the Corrie to Brodick road. I heard a fearful explosion. Looking seaward I saw an aircraft carrier which was obviously in terrible trouble. Black smoke was everywhere and I realised that I was

120

witnessing a horrible tragedy. On returning to duty in Greenock, I was informed, 'Something terrible had happened which could not be discussed as I had not been on duty at the time.' I asked if it was about the aircraft carrier blowing up, because if it was, I had actually seen it happen. They were all very surprised.

Ruby M Aitken

Ruby Aitken joined the Wrens on 10th March 1943. After training in naval store procedure in London, Ruby was drafted to HMS *Fortitude*, the wartime Armiralty name for the naval base at Ardrossan Harbour. The Wrens were billeted at Glenfoot House, a large imposing mansion on the outskirts of Ardrossan which was situated on the seafront overloolking Arran.

On arrival in Ardrossan on 29th March, the young Wren was told that an aircraft carrier had sunk offshore two days previously. No other information was given. All naval personnel were ordered not to discuss it with anyone. After the tragedy the seaside road was closed to the public as much debris and bodies were being washed ashore.

Later on the day of the funerals in Ardrossan, the flags that had been draped over the coffins were brought back to the naval store. As Rudy refolded and rolled them up, to place them back on their racks, flower petals were falling at her feet. Some days later Chief Petty

Ruby Aitken

Officer Briggs took Ruby into his office to carry out a most unpleasant duty. From a list in his hand he dictated the detials to the young Wren who entered them on consignment notes. Each note was sub-headed Coffin and Corpse, followed by names and addresses in the north of England. When the task had been completed the Chief Petty Officer emphasised that she must not tell anyone what she had just done. Ruby, who now lives in Port Bannatyne on the Isle of Bute, is still haunted by the memory of placing carbon paper between three sheets, two for depot and one for London & South Western Railway, who would be transporting the coffins. The towns involved were Newcastle, South Shields, Blyth, Doncaster and Sunderland. Her thoughts and sympathies were and still are with the families.

CHAPTER 10

THEY WERE NEVER TOLD

When the eyes of the modern reader see the words, aircraft carrier, an association is made. Aircraft carriers mean to us an advanced and sophisticated level of military, naval and aviation science. We see from recent conflicts in the Gulf, the Adriatic and such places where jet fighters and bombers, timed apparently to perfection, take off and land as if at will. Pilots appear to be skilled scientists and technicians as they interpret bewildering panels of dials. Every possibility seems to be covered by technology as another finely tuned jet speeds off on a mission with its smart weaponry. The organisation of the aircraft carrier itself impresses; teams of highly trained specialists seem to work in harmony to a common purpose. Their tools are the latest that technology has to offer. A mere shift in the breeze would be picked up and responded to by an array of radar and computer-controlled equipment.

But life on the Archer class group of escort carriers during the years of World War II was not like this. It will already be evident to the reader that sixty years ago things were very different and certainly a good deal less advanced technologically.

Nevertheless the naval authorities were not at all pleased with the outcome of *Dasher's* career, nor in the consequent loss of life. And in March 1943 the Admiralty were not only considering the loss of HMS *Dasher*. They also had the fate of her sister ship HMS

Avenger on their minds. *Avenger* had also been a cargo ship, hastily converted in America into an aircraft carrier. On November 15th 1942, when returning from Operation Torch, she had been hit by a torpedo, fired from the German U-Boat, *U155*. The torpedo caused an immediate fire on board *Avenger* and as the U-Boat Kapitan watched through his periscope, a massive explosion took place. The result of the terrible explosion led to the loss of the ship and the lives of 95% of the officers and ratings.

The loss of the two Archer class converted aircraft carriers, *Avenger* and *Dasher*, accounted for the deaths of over eight hundred British sailors and Fleet Air Arm men.

When the lease-lend agreement, which provided the ships, was signed between Britain and America, Winston Churchill was reported as having been advised that the Americans could carry out the conversions from cargo ship to aircraft carrier in six months. President Franklin D Roosevelt however stated that in America the work could be completed in three months. To prove their President to be correct, the American shipyards worked round the clock, seven days a week. It appeared that any short-cuts taken in the design and hasty conversion were being paid for heavily in British seamen's lives.

The board of enquiry into the loss of *Dasher* concluded their evidence in only two days. (Today such an enquiry into a disaster would take no less than six months.) On arrival at the Admiralty, the findings of the enquiry were studied by heads of departments during the first week of April 1943.

On April 6th an internal memo was passed from the Commission and Warrants Department. (The Commission and Warrants Department was a civilian-run department at the Admiralty whose function was to issue bulletins regarding promotions within the Royal Navy. During wartime they had the additional task of notifying sad news to the bereaved. During the war years they had the title CW Department (Casualties).)

The memo read,

Requesting information to pass to the grieving
relatives.

This department has little or no information on the disaster and ask Admiralty to note,

Next of Kin of casualties from 'Dasher' have been informed "Killed or missing, presumed killed on active service on 27th March as a result of an explosion on board the ship on which he was serving."

No mention is made of the name of the vessel or that she had been sunk.

We are being inundated with telephone calls from almost four hundred next of kin, all requesting information regarding their loved one.

We respectfully remind Admiralty that one of our own instructions is not being complied with, namely instruction C.A.F.O.2305/41, which reads, "As much information as possible shall be given to the next of kin of casualties at the time they are informed of their loss."

We are having a difficult time with relatives on the present meagre information we have.

A meeting of Heads of Departments, Admiralty, was held on 6th April, at which the loss of *Dasher* was discussed as well as the above memorandum from the Commission and Warrants Department. At the conclusion of the meeting, which was classified Secret, the following was determined:

The policy should be to withhold information that the ship has been sunk as long as the enemy is ignorant of this fact.

As,

a. The ship was sunk in sight of land.

b. bodies are being washed up, identified, buried etc. on the coast.

c. survivors have been picked up by a merchant ship and landed,

> it seems that the fate of the ship must be widely
> known and that it will not be long before the enemy
> hear of it.

Further discussed was the question of pensions and gratuities that may be due to the deceased or their next of kin. The political angle was also discussed. Questions about these American converted aircraft carriers were anticipated in view of the fate of *Avenger* and now *Dasher*.

At the same top level meeting, two further important questions were minuted as having been discussed: What additional information, if any, should be given to relatives now? The decision was that no additional information could be released 'at the moment'. And when could the announcement be made regarding the sinking of *Dasher*?

The conclusion to this latter question was that the news of the sinking of *Dasher* would be published as soon as the enemy is found to know, or in one month from date of sinking, whichever is earlier. The minutes were signed by JAS Pavis D.O.D.(h) and dated 6th April 1943.

From the minutes of this meeting we now know what the locals of Ardrossan knew, that bodies were being washed ashore. We also learn that it was at this meeting that the decision was taken that 'No information is to be released to relatives of the deceased.'

It is possible that because the Admiralty could not establish with any degree of certainty the cause of the explosion, they did not wish to release information.

However, the political context of this decision might bear some examination. At this time, plans had been set in motion to bring more than one million American troops to the safe waters of the Clyde during 1943. This signified a major involvement by the US in the war in Europe. These plans could have been placed in serious doubt if the Clyde's reputation as a safe haven had been called into question. A public announcement on the unexplained sinking of an American aircraft carrier with the loss of 72% of her British crew may not have been the kind of news that was considered politically advantageous. So it could be for these strategic reasons that every effort was made to ensure that information regarding the *Dasher* disaster was withheld.

Deep concern was being expressed in London about the lack of safety standards on *Dasher*. Recriminatory correspondence between the American Embassy and the Admiralty was causing a serious rift in British-US relations. When the disaster was classified Secret, no questions could be answered, blame could not be apprortioned and friendly relations between both Allied nations resumed.

The fact that relatives are still seeking information more than fifty years after the event shows the success of the policy of secrecy.

CHAPTER 11

WHAT COULD HAVE HAPPENED

After the findings of the board of enquiry had been received and studied by the Deputy Controller and his senior staff at the Admiralty, they accepted the findings and reported the following.

1. I have held a departmental meeting to consider the findings of the Board of Enquiry on the loss of HMS Dasher.

2. The findings of the board are concurred in generally and their picture of what happened so far as it goes is probably accurate.

3. There seemed little doubt that the explosion was a petrol vapour one. The sustained 'pouff' being consistent with such explosions. There was evidence of a 'detonation' type of explosion such as might be occasioned by depth charges or similar types of explosives.

4. From the damage sustained to the ship it is evident that the cause of the explosion was a large one consistent to a partial filling at least of the petrol compartment with vapour.

5. The causes of the presence and ignition of the vapour are not apparent, but may have been many, due to the inadequate safety arrangements in this class of ship.

6. As pointed out in my memo of 11 April, safeguards against accidents of this nature are, by our standards, practically non existent in the petrol arrangements and hangars of these American-built escort carriers. Steps have been taken to rectify this state of affairs but this will take time and will deplete our resources while rectification work is being carried out. Washington has been kept fully informed and asked to do what it can to get things rectified in new ships before delivery.

7. In spite of the fact that safety of these ships was low compared with normal carrier standards, the personnel do not seem to have been particularly trained nor special precautions taken. This has now been rectified.

8. Action has already been taken to cover all the other points raised by the Board of Enquiry.

Signed, Deputy Controller 30th April 1943

The evidence related to in paragraph 3 refers to a 'depth charge or similar type of explosion'. It has been ascertained that on board *Dasher*, in the stern area where the explosion occurred, there were ninety two depth charges and nine torpedoes stored in readiness for Atlantic convoy duty. A further fifty nine topedoes were stored in the torpedo room.

The Admiralty blamed the Americans for the disaster. The Americans in turn blamed the British. In a memo at the time the US authorities stated that the disaster was caused by,

'The lack of British experience with bulk aviation fuel.'

The level of official recrimination was high. Among ordinary seamen these escort carriers were already the subject of unease and ridicule. The already lost *Avenger* and *Dasher* – as well as the still operational and vital, *Archer, Activity, Biter, Battler, Hunter, Attacker* and *Stalker* – were known among the ratings in those days as 'Woolworth's Carriers'. At that time, Woolworth's stores sold very few items over the cost of six old pennies. Everything purchased from Woolworth's was cheap. Likewise it was the general opinion of those who built and those who served on these ships that everything was done 'on the cheap'.

Having received the board of enquiry report, the Commander in Chief of the Home Fleet sent out a secret memo to all other ships in *Dasher*'s class. Its contents, which were for immediate implementation, are worth quoting in full. They point to the cause of what went wrong and the great loss of life. The contents may have given some reassurance to the officers and ratings working on the sister ships under what must have been feelings of unease.

1. As a result of the investigations into the loss of HMS 'Dasher' it has been proved that the cause of the disaster was due to internal explosion, probably petrol.

2. Certain alterations to petrol stowage arrangements have been recommended.

3. The following immediate precautions are to be taken:–

(a)   The trunk giving access to the forward end of the shaft tunnel is not to be used.

(b)   The watertight door giving access from the Engine Room to the shaft tunnel is to be kept permanently closed.

(c)   Rigid observance of the magazine and petrol regulations is to be enforced.

(d)   All defects in petrol systems are to be reported to the Commanding Officer immediately they are discovered.

(e)   Commanding Officers are to ensure that the Engineer Officer in charge of the petrol system enforces rigid discipline in his organisation.

(f)   Smoking on the messdeck over the petrol hold is to be forbidden.

(g)   Particular attention is to be paid to keeping the bilges in the petrol compartment pumped dry so that the exhaust ventilating trunks are free from obstruction.

(h)   Life belts are invariably to be worn when ships are under way.

(i)   Calcium flares are not to be used in life floats, life buoys or life belts. Any calcium flares which it is desired to retain on board are to be kept in a watertight container.

This last precaution was included, it is thought, because a calcium flare may have been responsible for igniting the aviation fuel in the water. Those men who perhaps thought they had made good their escape from the sinking ship were then caught up in an inferno on the surface of the water.

As a result of the experience with *Dasher* the Royal Navy agreed to modify the petrol arrangements in these ships 'in accordance with normal British practice'. Acknowledging the amount of work involved and the time required to carry it out under a heavy programme of operational duties, a number of alterations were ordered as an interim measure.

Again quoting from the document signed by the Deputy Naval Commander and stamped 14th May 1943 is instructive of where it was believed that the problem lay.

. . . the following alterations are being undertaken as an interim measure.

(1)(a)   Reduce the amount of petrol carried to about 36,000 galls. The tanks not required for petrol to be filled with water and pipes blanked off.

(b)   Fit artificial exhaust ventilation to the hangar (inductor system).

(c)   Fit inductor ventilation to the petrol control compartment and cleavage gauge compartment.

(d)   Fit inductor ventilation to the petrol hold. (In 'Archer' and 'Biter' only).

(e)   Raise the general ship ventilation fans which are fitted in the hangar to positions as high as practicable above the 8' line. Fit spray shields to these fans.

(f)   Make doors leading to funnel uptake compartment, blower compartment etc. gastight.

(g)   Fit protective casing to exposed petrol piping on ships' side outboard.

(h)   Remove existing wiring from the cleavage gauge compartment and use magazine hand lamps pattern 8815.

(i)   Remove existing wiring from the petrol control compartment and fit exterior light box in accordance with British practice.

(2)   Fit asbestos fire curtains in the hangar as usual in British practice.

(3)   Blank door leading from engine room to shaft tunnel.

In a letter dated 19th May 1943, along with the board of enquiry report, the above information was sent by Sir Henry V Markham, Permanent Secretary at the Board of Admiralty to Captain TA Solberg in the office of the Naval Attaché at the American Embassy in London's Grosvenor Square. With those changes to be made 'in accordance with British practice' one can only wonder, with all the implied criticism of the Americans, just how it was received.

The minutes of the proceedings and the findings of the board of enquiry into the loss of *Dasher*, at this distance of time, may appear to give a plausible explanation of the catastrophe. Although far from satisfactory in any sense, at least a reason for death and destruction helps to explain. For most people whose lives were touched by these terrible events however, there was no such comfort.

All of the proceedings of the board of enquiry were conducted in secret. Even survivors had no means of knowing what had happened. The documents quoted here and elsewhere were only made available to the public in 1972. Talking to survivors in the writing of this book, it was evident that some had not even any clear idea who of their shipmates had survived and who had perished. Other seamen on the sister ships had no formal information to go on. All naval personnel were ordered not even to talk about the disaster.

The local population likewise had nothing substantial to help them interpret the events. Those who had witnessed the explosion or who had seen the casualties being brought ashore and even seen the funeral procession could only piece together such scraps of information that were to hand.

Some of the rumours and stories which circulated about the disaster and about the cause should be addressed. Many stories circulated throughout the length and breadth of Britain and these caused a great deal of distress to the bereaved, even more so, as they were unable to obtain information about the fate of their loved ones from the Admiralty.

Among the stories which are still alive to some degree are that *Dasher* was sunk by an enemy mine, she was the victim of friendly fire from a torpedo fired from a British submarine. The U-boat torpedo theory is still given credence in the minds of some, whilst others say it was a bomb planted on board. The 'blame-the-victim' explanation is still voiced, that the explosion was caused by a member of the crew smoking in a restricted area.

An Enemy mine

Although an enemy mine was thought to be unlikely – Ardrossan was the biggest minesweeping base in Scotland – according to a radio report a few days before the disaster, German planes may have dropped mines in the waters of the Firth of Clyde. The night before the explosion and sinking some locals on the Isle of Arran were walking in the company of Lt D McNair, when under cover of darkness they heard an unfamiliar drone of planes overheard. They decided the aircraft were German, possibly on a mine-dropping operation.

A Torpedo

A torpedo fired from an enemy U-boat would appear to be completely discounted as the extract from the German U-boat archives in Cuxhaven shows, 'No U boats were in the Clyde that day and records show that no U-boats were involved.'

The friendly fire story commences with the Deputy Controller

Stiftung Traditionsarchiv Unterseeboote

U-Boot-Archiv

Cuxhaven-Altenbruch, 22.09.1994

Mr. John Steele
104 Eglinton Road
Ardrossan
KA22 8NN
Scotland

Dear Mr. Steele,-

Thank you for your letter of 21st Sept.1994
and the enclosure of envelope for answer,- but no return-postage (see reverse side)

(I) To answer your request I enclose :

1. The british escort-carrier DASHER is destroyed at 27th March 1943 on the
2. River Clyde as a result of a petrol explosition and fire.
3. Ther was no German U-Boot near to that,- and no German U-Boot was involved.
4.
5.
6.

The German U-boat archive discount the involvement of enemy submarines

at the Admiralty who records in his memo dated 30th April 1943, 'there was evidence of a detonation type explosion.'

EC Traill, a survivor from Heswall in Merseyside, writes, 'In my opinion the ship was either mined or torpedoed.' Another survivor, RW Watts from Swindon, wrote in June 1996, 'To this very day I still maintain that we were sunk by a torpedo.' These two survivors were never called to the board of enquiry.

If it was a torpedo and it was not an enemy one, was it British? This would appear to be unlikely as the Admiralty have always denied that any British submarines were in the vicinity. However research shows that the training ship *Isle of Sark* was exercising in the vicinity with a British submarine.

Peter Tayler from Spalding, who served on board *La Capricieuse* records, 'We were involved in an exercise with a British submarine. HMS *Dasher* was four to five miles away.'

Now that it has been established that not one, but two British submarines were in the vicinity, is it conceivable that a torpedo was fired in error? Certainly another disaster almost occurred, when human error in the firing of a torpedo did in fact take place five months after the sinking of *Dasher*. The serious incident happened no more than twenty miles from the *Dasher* disaster site, at the Tail o' the Bank.

Many submarines were moored in the Holy Loch during their spells of duty. On returning to the loch from their very dangerous Atlantic missions, the safety procedure entailed a set of checks. One check was on the firing mechanism in the torpedo tubes. Prior to the safety check being carried out, all torpedoes were removed from the tubes.

Unbelievably one of the tubes still contained a torpedo with a live warhead. When the firing mechanism was activated, the live torpedo was dispatched straight towards Sandbank, the small town near Dunoon on the Cowal peninsula.

As it passed at great speed under many small vessels and even fishing boats in its path, eye witnesses could see the white wash from it, until it struck the shore with one almighty bang, sending sand, shells, water and stones high into the sky. Windows in dozens of houses were shattered and a huge crater was left, big enough to hold two buses. Fortunately no lives were lost. But what if an aircraft carrier had been in the path of the torpedo? What if the same thing had happened with the torpedo discharged southwards five months previously?

Engine Crank Case Blowing Up

Six of the ship's crew made the following observations at the board of enquiry –

> Lt Commander Lane's first thoughts were, 'there had been an explosion in the engine room boiler up-takes, as it was similar to previous explosions of that nature.'

> Lt Commander Wootton was in the engine room at the time of the explosion and he stated, 'It was a long explosion, similar to when the port engine crank case blew out.'

> Able Seaman Harold Martin said, 'It seemed like a boiler blowing up.'

Able Seaman Tom Hunter stated, 'It seemed like a blow back from the engine.'

Able Seaman George Reynolds was in the engine room and saw 'a flash coming along between the port and starboard engines.'

Ordinary Seaman Michael Dury said, 'I thought the explosion was from the engine room.'

Electrical fault

The board of enquiry ascertained that the lighting system was, 'not up to magazine lighting specification and that a fault in the system could have ignited petrol vapours when lights were switched.'

Metal to metal spark

The Admiralty were of the opinion that the safety of the American-built carriers was low and that the personnel were not particularly trained, nor special precautions taken. Due to this lack of safety training, did someone strike metal to metal causing a spark which could have ignited the petrol vapours?

Lt Commander Wootton saw the fire and flames shoot out from the bottom of the engine room after bulkheads. Many engine room personnel and other crew members witnessed the fire in the engine room. It would appear to be safe to assume that the engine room was on fire.

We also know:

1   the aircraft carrier had 75,000 gallons of fuel on board;
2   the aviation fuel tanks were full;
3   twenty four depth charges were in the hangar, twelve feet from the aircraft lift;
4   twelve depth charges were stored adjacent to the platform;
5   three torpedoes were stored on either side of the lift well, starboard;
6   three torpedoes were in the rack, portside;
7   all warheads were facing the stern of the ship (where the engine room is situated);

8   sixty eight depth charges were stored in a hatch, forward of the lift well;

9   the aircraft were being refuelled (immediately above the engine room);

10   the ship was fully laden with ammunition for the aircraft guns, the ship's 4" AA guns, four 40mm guns and eight 20mm guns;

11   there was a drip from the fuel tank. The drip was noticed two weeks before the explosion. It was never reported that it had been rectified. The rate of drip was once every five seconds (ie 12 per minute, 720 per hour);

12   six of the fuel tanks were situated in the engine room; the remainder were directly below; all tanks were full.

Lt Commander G W Dobson of *La Capricieuse*, Sub Lt ECD Holeman on *Dasher*'s motor launch ML528 and Leading Supply Assistant Harold W Baker all stated that they heard two explosions. If a second explosion took place, any one of the above, numbered one to twelve, could have been the cause.

A Bomb Placed On Board
Is it possible for this to happen, on an aircraft carrier, with more than 500 ship's company? At the board of enquiry into the loss of *Dasher*, over 40 questions were asked about 'unauthorised persons' or 'sentries'.

The last recorded questions were addressed to Lieutenant Commander E A Wootton. The questions and answers were,

> Question 559: 'During the time the ship was in at Dundee or in dock at Rosyth did any dockyard workmen go into the shaft tunnel or compartments adjacent to the petrol stowage?'
> Answer: 'No, Sir. It was not necessary.'
> Question 560: 'Were any special precautions taken to see that dockyard workmen did not go into unauthorised places?'

Answer: 'Adjacent compartments were locked, but to my
knowledge no sentries were specially detailed to watch
them.'

These two answers open up serious questions of security while the
ship was berthed in its last two ports, Dundee and Rosyth. Those
on board who would be privy to security arrangements would
include such a high ranking officer as Lieutenant Commander
Wootton, who as we now know, stated that 'To his knowledge no
sentries were specially detailed to stand guard over unauthorised
places.' Unauthorised places would be the bomb, torpedo, depth
charge, aircraft ammunition storage compartments, the 75,000 gallon
stowage compartment, and the aircraft aviation stowage compartment, containing thousands of gallons of high octane fuel.

In the three weeks it took for the repairs to be carried out in
Dundee, it would appear that civilian workmen and anyone posing
as a civilian workman, had the complete freedom to all parts of the
ship. Naval Intelligence in London must have considered the
possibility of a cunningly concealed time bomb.

That the authorities were at least aware of security and espionage
considerations is confirmed by the statement given by Mr Robert
Brown, a resident of Saltcoats.

'My father served in the first World War as a photographer
in the Royal Flying Corps. Most of his service was spent in
France. Then from 1919 till 1960 he managed his own
successful photographic studio. During the second World
War, he was involved in a great deal of photographic work
for the Royal Navy at HMS *Fortitude* (Ardrossan). One of his
duties was to photograph the survivors from HMS *Dasher*.
The reason for this was the fear that a German might have
slipped ashore posing as a survivor.'

Strange then, or more probably just naively lax, of the authorities
not to have proper security over access to the ship while in port.
Steps had been taken to pursue the possibility of espionage by the

enemy after the horse had bolted. Yet preventative security seemed not be have been in place. If the arrival of these escort carriers was considered to be so vital to the war effort in insuring against further losses of North Atlantic munitions and supply cargoes, it could be argued that vessels like *Dasher* would have been a target of German agents working udercover in Britain.

In researching this book, many people have contacted us to give their version of events. None have made more of an impact than a phone call and visit from the man who was the navigator on *Dasher* at the time. Lieutenant Philip Culmer was a career Navy man. In subsequent years he rose to the rank of Captain and was awarded a DSC with bar before retiring from active service in the late 1950s. Let the reader judge his recounting of an experience the night before HMS *Dasher* left Dundee, four days before the end.

'Sub-Lieutenant Langley, our Met Officer and a very conscientious young man, as Officer of the Day, carried out the customary rounds of the ship at 21.00 that evening. Such rounds always started or finished at the keyboard compartment where there was a sentry who held the keys of the keyboards themselves. Some keys could only be drawn by those on the list of authorised personnel and they had to be signed for in the keyboard log and the time entered. When the keys were returned the time was noted again and the sentry initialled that he had received the keys back. On this particular evening the sentry reported to Langley, "Keyboard not correct, Sir. The key to the bomb room is not on the board."

'Examining the log, the Sub-Lieutenant found the keys of the bomb room and also those of the bomb room lobby had been drawn during the afternoon and the signature for the keys was indecipherable. He then considered he should report to a more senior officer and finding the First Lieutenant not available, came to my cabin as I was Deputy Commanding Officer. Because of our early sailing for Rosyth the following morning, I was already in pyjamas and just turning in.

'Dressed again, I accompanied Langley to the keyboard flat. There we discovered the bomb room lobby key had been returned about an hour after it was drawn and the inference was that the key to the bomb room itself had probably been returned at the same time but not signed off. So a full examination of the keyboard was undertaken to see if it had been hung on the wrong hook.

'There still remained the question of the indecipherable signature and the keyboard sentry who had been on duty in the afternoon was sent for to find out who had drawn the keys. All he could remember was that he had issued the keys to a dockyard civilian who said a couple of valve wheels needed checking and he had been given authority to draw the keys so that this job could be carried out. The keyboard sentry described the civilian as a "well-spoken chap". When the sentry was told by this civilian that he had a meeting with Lieutenant Commander William Allan who was chief engineer on board and that to save time he had been asked to pick up the keys, he thought he should comply and issue them. The same civilian had returned some keys to him about an hour later and he had initialled them in. He had not noticed only half the keys drawn had been returned.

'Immediate instructions were given to the Coxswain to have the ship's regulating staff (ship's police) institute a search for the missing keys in the vicinity of the bomb room and lobby whilst I went and reported the matter to the Captain who by then had also turned in for the night. He approved of the measures being taken and instructed he be kept informed of any developments.

'Within half an hour the Coxswain reported back with the keys of the bomb room in his possession, saying they had been found in the bomb room lobby lying on the floor just inside the door, hidden by a ball of cotton waste. The Coxswain undertook to give a thorough rocket to the afternoon watch keyboard sentry for issuing keys to someone other than a member of ship's personnel authorised to draw them. A final report was made to the Captain and First Lieutenant and that concluded the incident.

'Later Lt Commander Allan was asked about this meeting and he denied all knowledge of having an appointment with a dockyard civilian that afternoon. Next morning early we were underway to Rosyth and amongst all the other demands the incident was forgotten.'

Clearly, this civilian workman with his well-spoken manner was not an authorised person to be given keys. He had unsupervised access to the bomb room and other areas below decks. It is not beyond the bounds of possibility that were he so disposed, this person could have planted a delayed action device which did its work some four days later when the ship had sailed around the north of Scotland to the Clyde estuary.

Plane Crash Whilst Attempting To Land On Board

There are eye witnesses from Ardrossan, West Kilbride, Seamill and the Isle of Arran who all support the cause of the explosion as being an aircraft crash. Alex Buchanan from Motherwell was a radar instructor aboard the training ship *Isle of Sark* which was involved in the rescue operation.

Alex wrote to a national newspaper that 'the popular theory on our ship was that one of *Dasher*'s aircraft had crashed on landing and had caused a torpedo to explode.'

PA Marsden of Southampton had joined *Dasher* at Liverpool in January 1943. He wrote to a local newspaper relating his experiences aboard the aircraft carrier. 'A Swordfish missed the flight deck when landing. It hit the quarter deck and caused the depth charges which were stored there to explode.'

The computer printout for HMS *Dasher* from the Wrecks Section, Ministry of Defence states, 'Sank following petrol fire and explosion thought to have been caused by an aircraft attempting to land on carrier.'

Father John Barry of North Berwick is compiling a manuscript entitled *Naval Battles that Never Were*. His research states,

'Two hundred and fifty naval personnel who had been transported to the United States to join ships of the Attacker class at Pascagoula Naval Yard on the Gulf of Mexico, heard a strong rumour about the sinking of *Dasher*. They heard that one of *Dasher*'s aircraft was preparing to land on the carrier at 1648 hours. The rumour was that the pilot misjudged his height on approach to the carrier and instead of landing on the deck, the plane plunged into the space between quarter deck and the flight deck.'

This would certainly have explained the 'muffled rumbling report' and the suddenness of the explosion. It would also have explained the smoke seen belching out between the flight deck and the quarter deck. Father Barry goes on,

'That such an accident could happen was proved on 1st April 1944 when an Avenger aircraft, having developed a defect in its depth charge sacks, was attempting to land on HMS *Tracker*. It missed the flight deck and flew straight into the round down. The aircraft burst into flames, setting off ammunition in the aircraft and round the ship's Bofors gun.

'Finally the aircraft engine fell onto the quarter deck, starting a dangerous fire. Safety precautions, newly installed, and efficient damage limitation prevented a repetition of the *Dasher* disaster.'

GJ Humphries from Hornsey, London, was on board LCT513 (Tank Landing Craft) attached to the 20th LTC flotilla. LTC *513* was lying at anchor north of *Dasher* and acting signalman Humphries was on the bridge, observing a plane approaching for landing. He records,

'I observed the *Dasher* and was interested in what she was about. I saw the plane going to land on her flight deck, but it crashed into the space between the flight deck and the quarter deck. I went quickly down to the wardroom to inform the commanding officer. No time was wasted in getting our craft underway. What I have related regarding the plane crashing onto the ship is perfectly true. I can see it happening even today.' (18th September 1996)

Allan S Davidson from Hornchurch in Essex relates,

'On Saturday 27th March 1943, I was 11 years and 10 months old and returning from a hike with the 1st Ardrossan Scout Troop. We were walking south east on the back road between West Kilbride and Ardrossan. The hill there is around 300 feet and the view was exceptionally clear and minute details of Arran could be distinguished.

'As we watched one of the planes come into land, someone commented that it appeared to be approaching lower than the previous planes we had seen. It appeared to go under the flight deck into the ship but we could not believe it and continued to see if it appeared further along the flight deck or from behind the bow if it had flown low on the far side of the ship. None of us saw any further signs of the plane and we were very puzzled and were discussing what we had seen when we noticed a wisp of smoke coming from the stern of the carrier. This rapidly thickened and as we watched, it became a plume of very thick black smoke and after a very short time the carrier sank.

'We sat there appalled and watched the boats attempting to rescue the surviving crew members until it started getting dark. We discussed the tragedy many times thereafter but never found out the cause. There is no doubt in my mind or in the minds of my companions that the aircraft we saw coming in to land that fateful day was too low and it went under the flight deck into the fuel tanks. Over the years, I have told this story to many people and I have never wavered in my conviction that the plane crashed into the ship under the flight deck.'

L.A.K. Boswell DSO, the captain of HMS *Dasher* was critical and outspoken about the safety aspects regarding his ship especially the walkway above the aircraft refuelling area. Captain Boswell had taken charge of the carrier only three weeks previously.

No one was allowed to smoke on board ship as there was always a strong presence of vapour fumes and it would take only a spark to set them off. Captain Boswell was extremely upset by the *Dasher* explosion and sinking, in part because he had vociferously voiced to his superiors his own strong concerns over the lack of safety on *Dasher*, and had felt he had been ignored. It seemed that the need to keep the ship operational, even if unsafe, to participate in convoy duty, was paramount.

After the sinking Royal Navy history was made when, as captain of the ill-fated vessel, he was not invited to attend the Board of Enquiry into the loss of his ship. Had he been given the opportunity he could have given extensive evidence regarding the official disregard of the known dangers on board.

Later, one of the ship's officers reported to Captain Boswell that he was walking along a walkway when he came across a rating smoking. When the rating saw the officer he hastily threw his cigarette down a venting tube which resulted in petrol vapours igniting followed by a huge explosion.

Other people who witnessed the drama from the Isle of Arran take the plane crash-landing view. Bill Spence and Bill Dickie were teenage boys in 1943. Bill Spence was a grocer for forty-two years and worked on Caledonian MacBrayne ferries for eight years. Bill Dickie became the island postman for forty-two years and is a Justice of the Peace. Like most other boys on an island community, they were shipping enthusiasts and they had gone down to the seafront that Saturday afternoon in 1943 to watch the nautical activity. They take up their story.

'We were watching the various types of vessels going about their business. Circling the aircraft carrier was a motor launch which must have been on duty as aircraft were flying off, then landing back on the carrier.

'This activity was of special interest to us, especially the planes. We watched one plane flying off, then it circled and approached the ship. It came very low, in fact it was below the level of the flight-deck. It flew towards the carrier and then disappeared. We assumed that it was flying past the other side of the ship at low level. We watched the bow of the ship for the re-appearance of the plane but it never came in view. Then we heard a deep rumble, followed by an explosion.

'The ship started to go down by the stern then it very slowly disappeared. A few seconds later, the sea went on fire. We just could not believe what we were witnessing.

'The rescue ships went as close as they could to the high flames and dense black smoke. We could not see anyone in the water, due to the distance. However by the activity of the various rescue vessels, we knew that a major operation was in progress.

'Both of us firmly believe it was the low flying plane that had crashed into the ship, beneath the flight-deck, which had been the cause of the sea disaster.'

CHAPTER 12

PRECIOUS MEMORIES

When Britain was in a state of conflict and our young men were fighting in a war zone, families and sweethearts were thinking of their loved ones, silently hoping for their safe return home. When the fighting men were known to be in the comparative safety of British territory, relatives probably felt that bit safer. Imagine the complete devastation then, produced by the curt telegram sent to 356 families which read, DEEPLY REGRET TO INFORM YOU _____ IS MISSING ON WAR SERVICE ON 27TH INSTANT. A further 23 families received a further telegram informing them of funeral arrangements.

Each young sailor left behind many broken hearts. Although most were lost without trace or explanation, the memory of many of them still lives on. We have been privileged to share a few of these precious memories.

William JR (Richard) Tomblin, Coder

Richard Tomblin

Richard was employed in the offices of London and Westcliff Properties until joining the Navy in 1940. His brother Eddie also took up a Naval career. Fate was to bring the two brothers together after a long absence. Eddie's ship was moored at Weymouth and he was ordered to take two guards and escort a prisoner from Weymouth to Portsmouth.

It was an offence during war time to post letters whilst ashore, thus avoiding the censors. A young sailor had been apprehended doing so and was sentenced to five days in the cells at Portsmouth. When Eddie arrived to take this young sailor under escort he was shocked to see that it was his brother Richard. 'I was only posting a letter to our mother,' Richard told him. This was the last time Eddie was ever to see his brother.

Richard's two best friends aboard *Dasher* were John Melville and Cecil Davies who were both killed in the disaster and buried together at Ardrossan Cemetery. Many years later John Melville's daughter Isobel, when sorting through her dad's belongings came across a photograph with the name Richard written on the back. Realising that he must have been a close mate of her dad's she forwarded the photograph to John Steele who was in the process of writing his first book *The Tragedy of HMS Dasher*. This photograph was published in the book stating 'Richard. Surname unknown, a shipmate of John Melville.'

In 1996, a year after the book was published Eddie's daughter was on holiday taking a bus tour round the Scottish Highlands. During one of the stops whilst browsing in a book shop she spotted the book, *The Tragedy of HMS Dasher*. The name seemed familiar and she remarked to her husband, 'I think that was the ship that Uncle Dickie was on.' On opening the book she was utterly speechless to see the photograph of her uncle. After purchasing the book, she could not wait to get home to give it to her dad.

Eddie still had his brother's five medals, which had been awarded posthumously. Now that he knew where the *Dasher* had gone down taking his brother Eddie with it, he was determined to bring three of the medals to the scene of the disaster. On Monday 12th August 1996 Eddie brought the medals to show John Steele, then

Peter Roberts

1942, when serving on the motor gun boat, Peter was Mentioned in Dispatches for bravery during an encounter with the enemy. This honour was published in the *London Gazette* on February 10th, 1942.

Although Peter was a busy lad he found and married a lovely Belfast girl. He looked forward to the end of hostilities when he could bring her home to meet all the family. Alas this was not to be as Peter's career came to an abrupt end when he joined the ill-fated *Dasher* and was one of the many boys lost to the sea.

In 1996 the *Sunday Post* newspaper published a small article about the *Dasher* book to which Peter's brother Ronald replied. A short time later Ronald received a phone call from Belfast. He just could not take it in when a voice said, 'I think you are my Uncle Ronald.' Could it really be true? Peter's wife had given birth to a son and they had not known of his existence. What rejoicing there was when the family all met up in Blackpool in the summer of 1996 to welcome Kenneth into the family after all of these years.

Peter's brother Arthur always remembers the last time he met up with Peter. In February 1943 when the *Dasher* arrived at Dundee the two boys were able to get together.

Peter was awarded post-humously the 1939-45 Star, the Atlantic Star, the Africa Star with North Africa clasp and the War Medal.

together with his wife Edna boarded the Ardrossan to Arran ferry. As the ship passed over where *Dasher* lies Eddie, with tears streaming down his face, threw the medals into the sea saying, 'These are yours, Richard.'

Leading Telegraphist Peter Roberts

Peter was born in Montrose, Scotland on November 17th 1919. His parents were Jessie and Peter. He had three brothers and one sister. They were Kenneth, Ronald, Arthur and Ann. He attended North Links Primary School and Montrose Academy. An easy going chap, he was well liked and very sociable. On leaving school Peter decided to make a career in the Navy and he joined the boys' service on 2nd January 1935. He was only 14 years of age.

Peter had a very exciting and varied naval career during which he served on a battleship, cruiser, destroyer, anti-submarine motor boat, motor gun boat and the aircraft carrier, HMS *Dasher*. In

Frank Scragg

Acting Air Artificer Francis (Frank) H Scragg

Frank was born on May 16th 1923, the eldest of two sons of Charles and Gwladys Scragg of Llandudno Junction. He was educated at Broad Street School and John Brights Grammar School. He always did well and on a very regular basis was top of the class.

On leaving school he joined the Royal Air Force as he was very interested in flying and engineering. After being transferred to the Fleet Air Arm Frank was involved in servicing the squadron's aircraft. On completion of his day's work, he enjoyed a test flight with the pilot to check that all was well with the plane. On many occasions he flew over the Clyde estuary on test flights. Whilst attending a course at Keele University Frank met his future wife, Sybil, much to the disappointment of one or two of the local girls from Frank's home village.

Frank had served on HMS *Victorious*, but when he joined *Dasher* he always said that it was a floating coffin and that if anything hit the ship it would sink.

After the disaster Frank's parents received the telegram reporting him as Missing in Action. His 18 year old wife Sybil was pregnant, but lost the baby when told the devastating news. They were never told any details. A few weeks later when Frank's mum was in a local shop, the shopkeeper enquired if any news had been forthcoming. Frank's mum replied sadly, 'No we only know he was on the *Dasher*.'

Standing unnoticed in the shop was another local lad, Amos. By an almost unbelievable coincidence Amos had been on board one of the rescue vessels, the *Lithium*. He therefore knew all the circumstances surrounding the loss of *Dasher*, but as he had been told by the authorities not to talk about it, he didn't speak out about it to Frank's mum. He just stood silently waiting to be served in the shop.

Frank's mum never got over the loss of her son and changed from being a jolly happy person to a shadow of her former self and sadly died aged only 53, still never having been told.

The incident in the shop only came to light 47 years later in 1990 when Frank's brother Wilfred, while out walking in the country, met by chance, Amos, who recounted the story to him, saying that he was so sorry but he could not speak out against orders. Sybil, Frank's wife died in 1995, never ever knowing what had happened to her husband.

Petty Officer Stephen George Pile

Stephen was born on March 4th 1905. When he joined the Fleet Air Arm his family comprised of his dad Walter, his mum Sarah, two brothers Walter and Joe, two sisters Grace and Amy.

Stephen George Pile

Stephen married Louisa on 23rd December 1930 and they had a son Stephen and a daughter Maureen. Stephen joined *Dasher* in Brooklyn and when his ship arrived in Britain he made his way home to be with his wife and family. His daughter Maureen was thrilled to be presented with pretty little dresses her dad brought from America.

When his son and daughter saw his suitcase lying open on the chair beside the living room door they knew their dad was home. On one of his last leaves Maureen sat on her dad's shoulders, dangling her feet, whilst combing his hair.

On Christmas Eve 1942 Stephen was expected home and all the family, including his mother, were watching out for him. As they looked out of the window they saw him come running over the hill. The moon and stars were so bright and the thick snow was sparkling on the ground. A happy memory never to be forgotten.

When the Missing Presumed Dead telegram arrived at the family home life seemed to come to an end. Stephen's wife Louisa very seldom spoke about her husband after that and when she did it was with a voice full of emotion. Because the Admiralty never released any information Louisa always waited, just in case Stephen came home. In 1975, Louisa died still waiting.

Signalman William A Speirs

William was born in London on March 31st 1921. He was named after his father and his mother's name was May. The other member of the family was his sister, May Dorothy. As a young child the family moved to Chadwell Heath, Essex. After he finished schooling he started his career with a printing company. When war was declared he joined the First Aid Division of the Civil Defence Organisation, where he carried out his duties until being called for service in HM Forces. In 1942, he joined the Royal Navy at Chatham where he trained as a signalman. In June of that year he travelled to the USA and on 1st July he boarded HMS *Dasher*, his first and only ship.

William Speirs

William's sister, May, served in the Woman's Royal Naval Service from April 1943 until March 1946, with HMS *Raleigh*, situated in Torpoint, East Cornwall. William's mother spent the last fourteen years of her life with her daughter and son in law in Winnipeg, Canada, where she died aged 96, still not knowing the details surrounding the loss of her son.

Jimmy Clayton

Leading Seaman James (Jimmy) Clayton

Jimmy lived in a small village by the name of Copy Crooks, near Shildon, County Durham. He had two sisters and a brother who was in the Enniskillin Dragoon Guards. After moving to Colchester he decided to join the Royal Navy. On completing his training at HMS *Ganges*, he served on board four ships before joining HMS *Cornwall*. He was out in the Far East when the war commenced and his ship was engaged in battle with a German sea raider in the Indian Ocean. Jimmy was awarded four medals prior to joining *Dasher*.

Supply Assistant George Bruce Irvine, Fleet Air Arm

George (Doadie) Irvine was born on August 4th 1913 in Ivy Cottage, Charlotte Street, Lerwick, Shetland Isles. The family comprised of mum, dad, 2 brothers and 4 sisters. Being a Shetlander he was always very interested in boats and boating. In his younger days he enjoyed model yachts and competing in regattas. This of course developed into bigger boats and he was soon the proud owner of a Shetland model racing boat and competing in major regattas

George worked for thirteen years with D & G Kay, Grocers, Lerwick. He was an extremely popular shop assistant, a great favourite with the customers. He attended Lerwick United Free Church where he was a member of the choir. He attended services and choir practice on a regular basis.

In his spare time George enjoyed the open air life which included cycling, sailing and camping. He was also a keen observer of nature, especially the bird life of the islands. On August 8th 1940 George married

George Bruce Irvine

Margaret (Manga) Thomson and their only daughter, Irene was born in October 1942.

When hostilities commenced and call-up came, it was natural that the navy was his first choice. George was home on leave and had returned to his ship ten days before the telegram arrived with the terrible news that he was Missing in Action. Two weeks later when the second telegram arrived stating that he must be Presumed Lost, the *Shetland News* reported the sad news about George, son of the late Mr GT Irvine, in the war casualty list. The report concluded that, 'He was an exemplary young man who was highly respected and much loved by all who knew him.'

George Benjamin Bowles, Scullion

George was born in East London on June 22nd 1921 and lived with his widowed mother, three sisters and three brothers. They

George Bowles

Jack Rockliff

were Olga, Sarah, Joan, Edmund, Charles and Leonard.

George left school at the age of 14 and was employed at the General Post Office as a messenger boy. He then moved on to a firm of cabinet makers in the City of London to learn the art of French polishing. When war was declared the business closed. George then commenced employment in the building trade, helping to repair war-damaged properties.

He was a member of the Territorial Army but at his call-up medical he was declared unfit for the army. George was then encouraged to apply for service in the Auxiliary Fleet by two of his friends who were already in the service. He applied, was accepted and served on HMS *Dasher*.

He was due home on leave when his mother received the telegram stating that he was Missing Presumed Killed in a mystery explosion. George's

mother died at the age of 86 never knowing exactly what happened to her eldest son.

Ordinary Seaman John (Jack) Rockliff

Jack was born in Barnsley on November 13th 1922. Unfortunately his mother died when he was only three years of age. From then, he and his sister Connie became very close, they both got on very well. He was a very happy lad who played for the school football team. During one of the matches he broke his leg and it was his sister Connie, who pushed him around in a wheelchair, to enable him to attend the matches as a spectator. Jack was always doing something. He was a very good scholar. On leaving school he enjoyed a game of snooker. He was classed by the ladies as a lovely dancer and was an avid Bing Crosby fan.

He started work in a local glass factory in Barnsley and

worked shifts producing bottles. As he grew older, he had a lovely young lady friend and they were planning their future together. However this was not to be as when war broke out, Jack joined the navy and was posted to HMS *Ganges* for training, at the completion of which he was posted to *Dasher*. When Jack was on his last leave he told his family the ship was tied up with a piece of string and it was not seaworthy. Ever since the heart-breaking telegram arrived, Jack's father always maintained that when the officers and men embarked on *Dasher*, they might well have said that they were in their future coffin.

Able Seaman Bertie Wilfred Griffin

Bertie was born on February 2nd 1911 in Walthamstow, East London to Ada who was a milliner and Bertie, who was a carpenter. He was the fourth child in their family of six. He had three older sisters, a younger sister and brother. The family lived in Gamewell Road, Walthamstow, opposite the local school which all the children attended. In the mid twenties the family moved to Chingford on the Essex border. After much studying, Bertie qualified as an accountant.

He was a very good tennis player, playing at club level and he was well known as a very popular fun-loving person.

On joining the Royal Navy in October 1941, Bertie was posted to HMS *Ganges* and on

completion of his course was posted to the Isle of Man for further training, at the end of which he came out top in his division and joined a corvette which had a Norwegian crew. In June 1942, he was in New York to join *Dasher*. During his navy service, Bertie corresponded a great deal with his older sister, Florence.

Florence had a boy, Derek and a girl, Doreen. Both adored their Uncle Bertie and when he was home on leave he always made sure that he spent plenty of time with them. They had much fun together as he was a great story teller and the proud owner of an adorable golden cocker spaniel called Punch.

Twelve days before the terrible tragedy, Bertie was home on leave and wrote a letter to Florence, his favourite sister. His last letter is dated 15th March 1943 and reads,

Dear Florrie,

I know it is quite a long time since I last wrote but I have had enough of being at sea and no communication anywhere. Everybody is complaining that I never write and when they do, eventually get my letters they may get a packet, if they are not lost.

Anyhow I have just had a few days leave and was not too late to send you a telegram on your birthday. Hope you received it on time. I am always thinking of you and the children and I carry their photographs with me.

I don't know if I let you know that we were in at the North African invasion from the start and were initially responsible for the capture of Darlan the Perisher. (Darlan was a Vichy French Admiral) It was fast and furious while it lasted but quite exciting. I have now just returned from I believe hunting the Eugene and the Tirpiz but we never know just enough. The old ship has returned for repairs after encountering that awful gale in mid February. Can you imagine wind velocity of 108mph in a temperature of 25⁰ below freezing point? Anyhow it was good to get back.

I have had a good leave and return tomorrow. Please write whenever you can spare a moment. Good luck to you and the children and kind regards to all and of course love and kisses to Lily.

Bert.

Lieutenant Fleetwood Elwin Price, Gunnery Officer

Fleet, as he was known to all, was born on 20th January 1901 in the family home at Harringey Road, Tottenham, London. On leaving school he joined the navy as a midshipman and was posted to HMS *Knight Templar*, an armed merchant cruiser in July 1918. When this ship was laid up in December 1918 he was posted to HMS *Sunhill* on which he served until early 1920 when he was demobilised.

Lt Fleetwood Elwin Price

Between the wars, Fleet worked for Spicers, a paper manufacturing firm in London. He married Olive in the early 1930s and they had two daughters, Monica and Thelma.

He again volunteered for the navy in May 1940 and after appearing before a selection board on June 4th he was appointed Sub Lieutenant and began his training the following month. A few weeks later he was posted to HMS *Montclare,* another armed merchant cruiser, which he joined on August 12th, 1940. His service on this ship lasted until May 1942. During this time the ship travelled in convoys between Bermuda, Halifax-Nova Scotia and Reykjavik.

In June of that year he was posted as gunnery officer to *Dasher* and with other crew members he joined the ship at the American Navy Yard at Brooklyn on July 2nd. Fleet served on *Dasher* throughout its short life and when she blew up and sank he was picked up by the *La Capricieuse*, one of the ships involved in the rescue operation. Unfortunately Fleet died of his injuries shortly after being plucked from the cold water. He was buried with five others in Greenock Cemetery.

Able Seaman John (Jackie) C Walker

Jackie was the only child and adopted son of James and Elizabeth Walker. Despite extensive searches of Registry Offices over a wide area no record of his birth can be found. His birth name is not known and there appears to be no record of the adoption nor of any baptism at the local Sacred Heart Church. He was brought up at 129 Dundas Street, Grangemouth and attended the Sacred Heart Primary School, Kirkintilloch where his name appears on the War Memorial in the entrance hall. He was enrolled in class 1C on August 24th, 1931.

During his school years Jackie befriended Frank Boyle. They were both scouts with the 61st Stirlingshire Scout Troop and attended the summer camps together. On leaving school he started an apprenticeship with Mr Baird, Slater and Plasterer. When Jackie commenced his apprenticeship he would take Frank with him on various jobs where Frank would assist by mixing the cement or plaster. Together they spent a lot of time climbing up on the roofs to replace slates and tiles. Jackie

Jack Walker

was extremely popular with everyone for his cheerful outgoing character. He was very good looking, always joking, whistling and singing. He was also gifted with a lovely tenor voice. A fine sportsman and a good footballer, he played for the scout team.

In his late teens, Jackie joined the Royal Navy Volunteer Reserve. As a result of this he immediately entered the service at the outbreak of war in 1939.

His adopted father died on July 16th 1946, the grave at Grandsable Cemetery, Grangemouth is marked by a plaque. The inscription reads,
J S Walker.
Dear Husband of E Henderson.
Also Jack, Our Dear Son.
Lost at Sea 27 March 1943.

Owen Johnstone (left) with this older brother Robert in 1935, aged 12.

Owen died in the Dasher disaster. His older brother was in the Fleet Air Arm and he was killed seven months earlier

Sub Lieutenant Owen Temple Johnstone

Owen was born on 6th June 1923 to Lawrence and Hilda Johnstone. He had an older brother Robert and two sisters, Margaret and Francis. He joined Roslin House Prep School, in Felixstowe, Sussex in 1930 and remained under the care of Sir Willes Chitty until 1937. A school friend recalls he was a quiet lad but fascinated by all types of boats, hence he was given the nickname, Boats. When the family were all at home they always took the opportunity to go boating together on the River Deben, Old Felixstowe.

Owen's brother Robert was in the Fleet Air Arm and kept his young brother enthralled with all his exciting stories. This gave Owen the ambition to also join the Fleet Air Arm.

After prep school he was off to join the Naval College at Dartmouth. On leaving college he was a happy lad to attain his ambition to join the Fleet Air Arm. Sadly he lost his life on the *Dasher*. The family suffered a terrible double loss as Robert had also been killed. Both boys were lost within seven months of each other.

Two young brothers lost their lives during active service in the Royal Navy. But their parents never understood why they received only one letter of condolence for Robert which also explained the circumstances of Robert's death. Regarding Owen, despite asking many questions they were never told.

In the mid-sixties their father Lawrence Johnston dedicated a stained glass window in the church of St Martin, Trimley, near Ipswich, Suffolk to the memory of his two beloved sons.

Able Seaman Sylvester (Syle) Woolaghan

Sylvester was born on April 14th 1918. His mother Catherine was

156

born at Salter, near Enerdale Lake. He was named after his father who was a coal miner at Cleaton Moor. Sylvester had one brother James and two sisters Winnifred and Mary. They all attended the same school, St Josephs, Frizington, Cumbria. This was the same school that their mother had attended.

On leaving school he worked in the Salutation Hotel, Ambleside, in the Lake District. His brother followed in his father's footsteps by working underground in the mines. Sylvester married a lovely girl from Liverpool prior to joining *Dasher*. Much to his surprise one of his friends, William (Billy) Barnes from the next village was also a member of the *Dasher* crew.

When the dreadful telegram arrived at Sylvester's home it stated that the funeral would be held in Ardrossan. Sylvester's father and his mother's sister travelled to Ardrossan. His mother was so overcome by grief that she could not travel to Scotland. On arrival, they requested that the body should be taken to Frizington for burial. The Royal Navy were reluctant to comply with their wishes. However Sylvester's father and aunt insisted and the Royal Navy agreed. After attending the funeral for twelve of his shipmates in Ardrossan his father and aunt returned to Frizington to arrange the funeral service which was held in St Joseph's Church, after which Sylvester was buried in the church grounds. Sylvester's parents' home was opposite the church and every night his mother opened the front door and said a prayer for her son. Until the day she died his mother wore black and every year when she inserted a notice in the local newspaper in memory of Sylvester she always included in the notice, Billy Barnes, whose body was never recovered. Sylvester's wife returned to her home town of Liverpool.

Sylvester's sister and most of his cousins reside in Australia. One of his cousin's, Mary Smith still resides in Frizington and attends to Sylvester's grave.

William (Bill) Gillies

Bill is remembered and still loved by his fiancée from all those years ago, Helen Ramsey of Edinburgh. Helen recalls how when she met Bill he was employed by W & A Gilbey, Wine Merchants, Haymarket, Edinburgh. In April 1939 he got his militia papers then left Edinburgh in October 1939 after the outbreak of war. He was posted to the Royal Naval Air Station at Pitreavie in Fife, before joining the *Ark Royal*, on which he spent fifteen months in the Mediterranean. When his ship was sunk in November 1941 Bill was given 32 days survivor's leave before joining the *Dasher*. Bill didn't like the *Dasher* and claimed no one was happy on it. He was never to come back.

Helen remembers Bill as a kind, thoughtful and considerate boy. He was dux of his school and won the Heriot Watt College medal. Bill loved life and led it to the full always busy playing tennis or hill walking. Later when Helen went to the National Shrine to see his name on the Remembrance Stone she could not find it. On enquiring of the Master-at-Arms she was informed that because Bill had been born in Calgary, Canada his name could not go on the Shrine. This was extremely upsetting for Helen as Bill had lived in Edinburgh since he was four years old. He had served his country and paid with his life.

Since losing Bill, Helen has continually asked the authorities for details but has been met with a wall of silence. Helen has never married and still says, 'Bill was one of the best.'

Acting Leading Airman Roy Eric Levick , aged 19 told his mother before leaving home to rejoin Dasher, *'This will be my last leave. I will not survive.'*

Stanley Cyril Voice
Leading Air Fitter

Born 1920 in Shepherds Bush, London, Stanley joined the Gas Light & Coke Company (Watson House) in 1936 as an apprentice gas fitter. After WW2 commenced, he volunteered to join the Fleet Air Arm and was sent to America to be ready for the commissioning of HMS *Dasher*.

Stanley did nor survive the *Dasher* disaster. His mother and father died knowing nothing about the circum-stances of his death other than a telegram

stating he was "Missing" and later another telegram stating "Presumed killed".

Stanley Voice, 2nd from left

CHAPTER 13

HEROES OF HMS *Dasher*

On studying the report of the board of enquiry into the loss of *Dasher* it becomes clear how members of the crew reacted in the chaos following the explosion. With every light extinguished, many fires starting and the vessel listing heavily by the stern, those on board knew immediately that their ship was sinking and that there were only a few desperate minutes to escape. In times of crisis, heroes emerge.

The following are a few of the brave deeds that have been uncovered. There must have been many other heroes aboard whose stories will never be told.

Petty Officer Jack Verlaque Jack Verlaque from Paisley led many young ratings to safety. Jack could have made his way quickly, on his own, but he decided to help others by leading them through the dark corridors to a point where they could jump off the ship.

Lt Commander E W E Lane On being ordered by Captain Boswell to find out what was happening, he made his way down to the engine room. The further down he went, the more damage, heat and danger he encountered. One deck was three feet under water, with the sea pouring in.

Realising that he could go no further he retraced his steps along the darkened passages to the deck. As he made his way to safety he stopped and checked every office and cabin on his route, to ensure that they were empty.

On jumping overboard he swam about the survivors in the water and in the Carley rafts shouting encouragingly with the words, 'It will be alright lads. We will soon be out.'

When a rescue boat arrived on the scene the crew threw ropes to those in the water. However, due to the coldness of the sea and the length of time in the water, the survivors' hands were numb and covered in oil. As a result they were having difficulty grasping and holding onto the ropes.

Lt Commander Lane swam about tying a bowline knot onto the ropes, thereby ensuring the struggling could hold onto the ropes or put them over themselves and be pulled towards the rescue vessels.

The Lt Commander risked his life when checking the offices and cabins prior to jumping overboard.

Whilst in the water he risked his life swimming about the Carley rafts shouting words of encouragement.

He could have boarded a rescue boat but instead he remained in the water tying knots in ropes to save others.

Heroes in the Mess Decks The crew members 'formed an orderly queue' to go through the watertight doors and make their way to safety, whilst the ship was in darkness and sinking by the stern. By acting in this manner with no sign of panic, these men upheld the highest standards in keeping with seafaring traditions.

Daniel Gaffney Whilst in the water, Daniel Gaffney from Glasgow, pulled an unconscious shipmate towards a raft. Then with the assistance of an airman, swam over to another injured crewman and brought him alongside a raft.

Petty Officer Jeff Gray On jumping into the water, Jeff Gray made for a Carley raft which was furthest away thereby enabling his shipmates who were not such good swimmers to make for the nearby rafts. Whilst swimming in the water, he and another crew member assisted a rating who had been injured, by swimming over to him and assisting him to the raft. On reaching the raft, they both helped the injured seaman to board the raft, after which Petty Officer Gray boarded and cradled the casualty's head on his lap whilst they were waiting to be saved.

There is no doubt that but for Petty Officer Gray's action, the seaman would have perished.

Captain J F Terretta and crew of SS *Lithium* The SS *Lithium* was owned by Imperial Chemical Industries Limited, Fleetwood. During her passage from Glasgow to Llandulas, Wales, SS *Lithium* was a quarter of a mile away from *Dasher* when the explosion took place. A bright flash appeared and dense smoke issued from the stern.

Captain Terretta turned his ship around to render what assistance he could. The captain and his crew saved sixty men from a watery grave. The men were then placed aboard HMS *Sir Galahad*. At 18.30 hours the SS *Lithium* having disembarked the survivors, proceeded on her voyage.

Captain Templeton and crew of SS *Cragsman* The flotilla of Royal Navy rescue vessels was stopped at the perimeter of the dense smoke amid searing flames when they witnessed the *Cragsman*, a small coaster built in Paisley in 1924, disappear into the billowing smoke. Fearing the worst for the coaster they were most relieved to see the *Cragsman* reappear laden with survivors.

At the conclusion of the rescue operation, the skipper and crew of the coaster transferred those they had saved onto a Royal Navy vessel. The *Cragsman* then slipped away quietly, to continue on her voyage.

Captain Templeton, from Londonderry, never reported taking part in the very dangerous rescue operation and his brave actions were never made known to the public or the survivors. His brave crew were James Warden, Londonderry; Joseph Maclean, Isle of Barra; Duncan MacRitchie, Ness, Stornoway; A Miller, Dalry; WJ Ferguson, Londonderry; J Aitchison, Ireland; Murdo Maclean,

Stornoway; James Bell, Paisley; Ian MacKenzie, Isle of Tiree; Duncan MacNab, Isle of Skye; R Dearney, Glasgow.

Lt Commander G W Dobson, *La Capricieuse* His lifeboats plucked twenty six survivors out of the sea. Unfortunately seven of them died by the time he berthed at Ardrossan.

Captain J H McNair Royal Navy, HMS *Isle of Sark* The *Isle of Sark*, a radar training ship, was four and a half miles from *Dasher* when she 'blew up'. On immediately turning towards her and heading at full speed, they watched as the aircraft carrier disappeared. Shortly afterwards a flame was seen followed by a big fire.

They saw two rafts with those on board paddling with their feet and hands to get as far away as possible from the flames.

Captain McNair stopped his ship just short of the 'sea of fire' and ordered his lifeboats to be lowered. At that point he witnessed a small coaster (the *Cragsman*) sail right into the smoke and flames to pick up survivors.

The *Isle of Sark* picked up thirty five survivors of whom three were unconscious. Artificial respiration was applied for some considerable time but the three could not be revived. Thirty two survivors were brought ashore at Ardrossan.

Sub Lt E C D Holeman RNVR (In command of *Dasher*'s motor launch *MV 528*) On witnessing the explosion and seeing the aircraft lift 'flying into the air,' he went to crash stations immediately, made toward *Dasher* and picked up a total of forty men, eighteen from the water and twenty two from Carley rafts.

Petty Officer John A Stamp Item number nine of the board of enquiry report reads,

> 'The behaviour and bearing of the officers and ratings was exemplary throughout. Petty Officer John Stamp RNVR assisted many young ratings to safety, but he lost his life in doing so.'

John Stamp whose bravery was mentioned at the board of enquiry and formally acknowledged many years later by Prime Minister John Major

It is recorded that John Stamp was making his escape when he heard cries of help from behind a jammed watertight door. Using all his strength he forced open the heavy door and managed to hold it open with his back while bracing himself with his foot against the bulkhead. Because John Stamp was a strong well-built lad he managed to hold this position to allow his shipmates to escape from the dark passageway behind the door.

At any point during this extremely brave deed John Stamp could have made his own way to safety but he choose to stay, therefore saving the lives of 'about twenty young ratings'.

In 1994, after a year of searching, a sister of John Stamp, Vera Marshall, was traced to South Shields. Another sister, Ann, and a brother, Alf were also found. They all have families and no one knew John had died a hero. The family were very grateful to be told the details. Alf Stamp had been trying for many years to obtain information regarding his late brother. They had never even been told where the *Dasher* had been lost.

With the full backing of all the family a campaign was set in motion to honour the name of the young Petty Officer who gave his life to save others. His sister Vera said, 'It will not only be an honour for John, it will be for all the *Dasher* lads who were lost.'

On enquiring of the government regarding the possibility of a posthumous medal being awarded, a reply received from Michael Portillo, Defence Secretary explained that in June 1946, the Interdepartmental Committee on the Grant of Honours, Decorations and Medals for the 1939-45 War decided that no further consideration would be given to awards for 1939-45 War service. Despite attempts over the years to reopen individual cases, all post-war governments have upheld this decision.

Although a medal would not be awarded to John Stamp it was felt that it should not be just accepted as so. After the publication of *The Tragedy of HMS Dasher* and the story of the brave Petty Officer became known, many people were of the opinion that something should be done. A petition for recognition was started in Ardrossan. Before long people were requesting forms to place in their local shops and clubs. The petition also circulated around Tyneside and even travelled out to five North Sea oil rigs. Letters of support were received from around the UK and from as far afield as Australia and Canada, asking for their names to be added.

When the Reverend KR Brown, a practising minister with the Methodist Church in Paisley, Scotland heard that no medals would be awarded, he felt so strongly about this decision that he forwarded a letter of protest to sixteen MPs. As the momentum grew Dr David Clark MP, Shadow Secretary of State for Defence contacted John Steele and invited him to present the petition to Downing Street.

In February 1996 a deputation comprising Dr David Clark, John and Noreen Steele, John Stamp's two sisters Vera Marshal and Ann Curran, handed in the petition to 10 Downing Street. Some weeks later, Vera Marshall was very proud to receive a letter of recognition from the Prime Minister, John Major. The letter is reproduced here.

Fifty three years after the terrible loss of life with the sinking of HMS *Dasher*, the British government had recognised for the first time one of the heroes who had been on board.

CHAPTER 14

THE SECRETS OF THE GRAVES

The *Dasher* disaster was classified as Secret and no information was released until 1972, when the *Dasher* file was placed in the Public Records Office in Kew. The fact that they were officially available to the public was never really known. No announcement is made to the press and the search of public records is generally a matter for journalists or researchers with a specific brief. As for the bereaved who persisted in enquiring of the Admiralty as to what had befallen their loved ones, they were never informed that the records were now available.

Those who did read the sad account of events surrounding *Dasher* were retired naval officers and professional researchers with knowledge of the system regarding classified documents being released.

In published books there would possibly be only a few lines regarding the demise of the aircraft carrier and the fatality list of 346 would be quoted from the official records.

Forty-nine years after the disaster, the Naval Historical Branch, of the Ministry of Defence in London, stated in a letter dated October 2nd, 1992, (Ref S10536),

'The casualty number of 346 was incorrect. 346 was in fact the number of Royal Navy fatalities. Other categories had been overlooked. Omitted for all of those years were 27 Merchant Navy personnel, 3 NAAFI personnel and 3 Royal Air Force personnel. The official casualty list should read 379.'

During the research for this book, it was ascertained that another overlooked situation required official clarification. There was an anomaly – the number of bodies brought ashore and washed ashore at Ardrossan exceeds those who were listed as buried by the Commonwealth War Graves Commission. The board of enquiry into the loss of *Dasher* records many naval witnesses quoting the number of bodies plucked from the Clyde. The total official number recorded by the enquiry is in excess of the number listed as buried.

It is recorded in an Admiralty document marked Secret, dated April 6th 1943 and signed by JAS Pavis, whose department was, in Naval parlance, D.O.D.(H). London. The wording in its entirety reads,

'Bodies are being washed up, identified, buried etc on the coast.'

Many residents in Ardrossan remember the public beach, known as the North Shore, being placed Out of Bounds and patrolled by Royal Navy personnel. This was because of bodies being washed ashore. The number of bodies brought ashore at Ardrossan and also the number of poor souls whose bodies were washed ashore locally over the following three weeks exceeds by far the number of known graves. Where are the missing bodies? Where 'on the coast' are they buried, as stated in the above letter and what do they mean by etc?

The staff of the Commonwealth War Graves Commission are highly respected for the manner in which they treat individual enquiries from those seeking information regarding relatives who perished during the years of conflict. However they could render no assistance to an enquiry to discuss the unknown graves.

Clarification was required as to the total number of unidentified bodies recovered and where they were buried. After a very lengthy telephone conversation, the War Graves Commission requested that our enquiry should be submitted in writing.

In section D Midwest of Ardrossan Cemetery, thirteen headstones stand in line (above), erected by the Commonwealth War Graves Commission Close by is another rectangular plot (below) which would normally accommodate fifty two plots. Only one naval headstone stands here. It is believed that one or both of these plots contain the missing bodies

Over the next eighteen months many letters and telephone calls were answered with reference to names on memorials. More letters and telephone enquiries confirming that it was not names on memorials that were being sought, it was the location of the unknown graves.

During this period, in an effort to trace graves of the unidentified, we visited every cemetery in Ayrshire and Renfrewshire. We checked the length and breadth of each cemetery for War Graves Commission Naval headstones in the hope of finding some of the missing *Dasher* graves. It should have been a simple matter to obtain the information from the Registrar of Births, Marriages and Deaths but the Registrar advised that during hostilities the Royal Navy were exempt from keeping records of burials of Navy personnel.

Searching through all the cemeteries could also have been avoided if details of burials of navy seamen had been recorded by the cemetery supervisors who are most meticulous in recording every detail of those buried. On checking the record books in all the cemeteries, it was noted that they reach back hundreds of years, with details of each individual burial carefully recorded. Every burial that is, except Royal Navy personnel during hostilities. No records were kept even at Ardrossan cemetery, where two funeral processions took place, each with full military honours.

On June 4th, 1996, a letter was received from the War Graves Commission which stated,

> 'Unfortunately no unidentifieds are recorded for *Dasher* casualties and we are unable to provide the information required.'

The letter further reads,

> 'There are 10 burials from *Dasher* in Ardrosssan Cemetery and 6 in Greenock Cemetery.'

Both of the above figures were in fact wrong. The correct numbers of burials in Ardrossan Cemetery are 13, not 10. In Greenock

Cemetery there are 7 graves, not 6. On cross-checking the names on the Graves Commission list, we advised them of the names and details of those who had been omitted. The two lists have since been ammended.

Visitors to the grave site at the Ardrossan cemetery were to note that headstones had been erected. Curiously though, two names had been engraved on each stone. Photographs exist to show this. After 1960 photographs show that each individual person had been given his own headstone by the Commonwealth War Graves Commission. In section D Midwest, thirteen headstones stand in line along the middle of a rectangular plot. Although in every other plot in the cemetery the headstones stand in double lines, back to back, the plot behind the *Dasher* stones remains unmarked. In total both of these plots could accommodate another sixty to seventy casualties. Situated close by is another large rectangular plot, the size of which would normally accommodate 52 headstones. But only one naval headstone stands alone on this plot, commemorating one World War I casualty.

Evidence strongly points to these two unmarked plots accommodating the missing graves. Although this cannot be verified without disintering any coffins in this ground, it would seem more than likely the plots contain the unnamed dead from the *Dasher*, laid to rest beside their shipmates.

The cemetery has been used to capacity and a new section opened. On enquiring of a cemetery official, 'Why not use these unmarked plots?' he stated, 'They are used up. I don't know who is in there as there are no written records, only word of mouth passed down through the years.'

A local witness, Bill Smith of Ardrossan, aged fourteen at the time of the disaster in 1943, remembers the tennis courts of Castle Craig, Ardrossan covered with either injured or dead on the Sunday morning (28th March). 'A large number was evident.' At the time his father was civilian security officer at Ardrossan harbour; his brother was a member of RNVR, also stationed at HMS *Fortitude*.

After the first navy funeral it would appear that the unidentified brought ashore were buried quietly. As more bodies were washed onto the beach, it would seem they were also buried quietly without notification to the relatives.

Under the circumstances it was probably an attempt to minimise publicity surrounding the disaster. A top level decision must have been taken to hold no more public funeral services. This would help to conceal the extent of the loss of life in the disaster and to maintain local morale.

The consequences for the bereaved relatives are, however, incalculable. Informed only that their loved one was Missing Presumed Killed meant that many were deprived even of the comfort of knowing that their kin were found and had been laid to rest.

CHAPTER 15

PREMONITIONS

Some of the crew members were never happy on *Dasher* **and** always felt ill-at-ease on the ship. Others were perturbed by the difference in pay between the Merchant Navy crew who were paid danger money whilst the Royal Navy crew were not, even although they were all on the same ship. One thing that few of them realised was that if their ship was ever sunk, the wages of the Merchant Navy crew were immediately stopped on the day of the sinking.

Bob Dotchin and another member of the crew who had joined the ship in Brooklyn were watching a worker welding the last internal sheet of metal. When the metal plate was finally welded into position, the workman, on seeing the two members of the crew watching him, burned the letters RIP onto the sheet of metal. He then stood up, turned round and walked away.

Whatever it was about the ship, many were uneasy, especially about the rushed conversion. Something always felt wrong and they spoke about their fears to their families and friends.

Prior to *Dasher* being officially handed over to the Royal Navy, Able Seaman Robert Watts from Penhill, Swindon, was stationed in Flushing US Naval Base, New York. One day Robert was part of a Royal Navy Guard of Honour at the opening of a new airport. As the mayor arrived for the ceremony, the rain began to pour down in a heavy torrent. Robert turned to his friend, Roy Walton and

Able Seaman Thomas Bretherton (right) with an unknown shipmate. When summoned back to Dasher *from home leave he became ill-at-ease and acted as if he knew that he would never return home again. He was reported missing presumed dead just a week later*

said, 'This is a bad omen. I bet we leave *Dasher* a damn sight wetter.' Within ten months, Robert did leave *Dasher* a damn sight wetter as one of the survivors.

When the storm-damaged ship arrived in Dundee for repairs, some of the crew were allowed shore leave. After being at home for a short time, many of them received telegrams instructing them to return to their ship the following day. This telegram caused a feeling of great uneasiness. Those on leave knew that the repairs required to the storm-damaged *Dasher* could not possibly have been completed in such a short period of time and the ship would not be seaworthy.

When Able Seaman/Stoker Thomas Bretherton received the telegram he became very quiet and ill-at-ease, not at all his normal self. On the day of his departure from home, Tommie turned to his sixteen year old brother Donald and said, 'Now look after mum and the kids and you can have my bike.' He kissed and hugged his mum before leaving. His mother was very worried about him, especially when she discovered that he had left his clothes behind, still in the drawer. On the shelf, he had placed his money and other personal items. His flask and lunch box were even left on the table.

Tommie's sister Joyce and his mum always believed that Tommie knew this was his last leave and he would not be returning home.

Jimmy Clayton from Copy Crooks, County Durham, was also, home on leave. His brother-in-law, Les Blades, looked upon him more as a brother and still has fond memories of him. Since leaving farmwork, Jimmy had served on three Royal Navy ships before joining HMS *Cornwall* which engaged in battle and sank an enemy sea raider in the Far East. He had been awarded the Atlantic Star and the African Star and Clasp.

Les recalls that Jimmy was home on leave when he received a telegram instructing him to join the crew of *Dasher*. On receiving the order to join *Dasher*, Jimmy told Les's mother, 'This will be my last trip. I have a feeling that I will not make it!'

Sub Lt Geoffrey Parkinson had a very strange dream the night before *Dasher* sank. He dreamt about the sinking in great detail, even to the extent that he would be rescued from the sea in the company of the cook and the captain. When he told his fellow officers the next morning it caused great amusement and they all reminded him that within twenty four hours they would all be on shore leave. However, when the ship did sink and Geoffrey was rescued from the water he was indeed on a raft with the cook and the captain, exactly as he had dreamt! Geoffrey survived the ordeal and made it safely home to tell his wife Mary of his disturbing dream. Geoffrey also told Mary of a second oddity that had occured when the captain was paying the crew their wages the day before, he insisted that every man should be wearing his identity disc. This was something the captain had never requested before. Geoffrey often wondered wether the captain had some sort of premonition. Strangely, of all the dead men Geoffrey had to identify, not one was wearing his identity disc.

Henry Charles Marston did not like the *Dasher* and did not want to be on board her but had no choice in the matter as no one could choose their posting. Harry kept repeating constantly to anyone who would listen, 'The ruddy ship is going to blow up. I am not going back.' When Harry's leave was up he was still of the same opinion. His wife Hilda contacted her brother Derrick, from Grantham, Lincolnshire, asking him to accompany them to the railway station as she was sure that Harry 'might do a runner'. To Derrick, Harry was not only his brother-in-law, he was one of his best friends.

After a lot of persuasion they managed to get him to the railway station and eventually onto a train. He was protesting all the time and at one point he took fright and jumped off the train. Hilda and Derrick were quite worried about the trouble he would get himself into and pleaded with him to get back on. Their pleadings were to no avail and Derrick managed to bundle him back on again. All the time Harry was still protesting.

Poor Harry had been right all along about *Dasher*. Hilda received the terrible telegram on her twenty-first birthday. Harry's distraught widow and brother-in-law could never erase from their minds the last terrible parting from Harry at the railway station.

Able Seaman George T Lovegrove, Cleveleys, relates, 'The night before *Dasher* blew up we were anchored in Lamlash Bay and I was in my hammock. I began to have an awful feeling that something terrible was going to happen. I went up to the flight deck and walked up and down the length of the runway. I just could not go back below as I had a feeling that the ship was going to sink. I knew that we were due to go on another Russian convoy and put my premonition down as a warning that this time we would not be coming back. I did not say anything to my shipmates and spent the rest of the next day in the mess deck.'

Tom Dawson was one of the fortunate ones who survived the disaster. Tom had been on duty at the ship's wheel when the explosion occurred. His girlfriend's brother, George Coulson was also a member of the crew but sadly he did not survive. Tom married his girlfriend and it was very many years later before his wife could bring herself to tell Tom that on that fateful day she had returned home from work to an empty house and settled down with a magazine. At approximately 4.50pm (the time of the sinking) she heard her brother's voice call her name. She assumed that he was home on unexpected leave and she searched the house. She learned the truth on the following day when her mother received the telegram.

CHAPTER 16

FLEET AIR ARM

The officers, petty officers and ratings all had their own specific jobs to do to ensure the smooth running of their ship. However aircraft carriers are different from other vessels as additional to the ship's crew, they also have on board all those involved with the aircraft. These are members of the Fleet Air Arm.

The aircraft crew on *Dasher* included pilots, observers and telegraphist/air-gunners. The maintainance crew (ground crew) were similar to those required in a Royal Navy air station and included, among others, air mechanics, air fitters, air artificers, radio mechanics and radar mechanics.

For all Fleet Air Arm personnel, everything was very different on an aircraft carrier compared to a naval air base. The pilots had the extremely difficult task of attempting to land on a runway much shorter than the ones in which they had carried out their training at a naval air base. The runway at the training base was much longer – up to four times longer – than that on an aircraft carrier.

During the practice landings at the base, a marker was placed at a point the length of the runway on an aircraft carrier. The Fleet Air Arm pilots practised landing their aircraft within the marker points. One of the advantages of landing at the base was that when the pilot landed and passed the marker, there was still ample runway to slow the aircraft and bring it to a halt. Also when landing at the base, the runway did not move, unlike the pitching and tossing of the short runway of *Dasher*.

When the aircraft were landing on a carrier, the arrester hook on the plane should make the correct contact with one of the arrester wires on the ship and bring the aircraft to an abrupt halt. On many occasions the arrester hook failed to catch an arrester wire. When this happened the pilot had no runway left in which to fly off. He and his aircrew faced the possibility of a lonely and watery grave as the plane shot over the side of the ship.

On convoy duty in mid-Atlantic, when a search was required for enemy U-boats, *Dasher* would pull out of the convoy and sail into the wind, to allow the aircraft to fly off, clear of all the convoy ships. After the planes had flown off, *Dasher* would immediately resume her place in the convoy.

The type of aircraft used were the Fairy Swordfish with a crew of three, pilot, observer and telegraphist/air gunner, or Sea Hurricane which were single seater aircraft.

For the air crew, the sighting of a periscope or conning tower in the wild wastes of the Atlantic was always a challenge. Their efforts proved very successful in discouraging U-boats from causing havoc to the convoys as they had done, to great effect, for too long.

The air searches were not always for the purpose of seeking out and destroying the U-boats. Sometimes a search was called to ascertain the position of a straggler, a ship that for one reason or another had fallen behind the convoy.

During the searches, the aircrew had to maintain radio silence throughout their two to three hour flights in the heaving Atlantic. At the end of the search it was always comforting for the aircrew to sight the convoy in its changed position. When preparing to land, the pilot would maintain enough height to clear the end of the flight deck and reduce speed. The nearer to the ship that the plane got, the more the pilot (and the air-crew) could see the up and down movement of the flight deck. The landings were always tense affairs with a feeling of great satisfaction when the hook caught one of the arrester wires, bringing the aircraft to an abrupt halt.

On board the carrier, the 'ground' crew worked in atrocious

weather and always in the most cramped conditions in order to ensure that the aircraft were maintained.

The Squadrons of the Fleet Air Arm were divided into Flights, each Flight comprising either three or four aircraft. The number of Flights and the length of time each Flight spent with *Dasher* was determined by the particular operations in hand.

When a Flight was posted from *Dasher* to another ship or a naval base, it was the custom for the Fleet Air Arm to hold a farewell party. This was by way of wishing good friends every success and the hope that some day they would all meet again. The following day the Flight would 'Beat-up-the-ship'. This entailed the departing pilots flying off, then flying over the ship as low as possible with their wings dipping and rising.

One day in the Clyde, after a lengthy farewell party, the departing Flight were demonstrating their skills. It was noticed that one of the pilots was flying particularly close to *Dasher* prior to the four aircraft departing into the horizon. The next that was heard of the skilful pilot was that he had made an unscheduled landing on a remote island off the west coast of Scotland and required assistance.

Aircraft Artificer George Chadwick joined *Dasher* in January 1943 at Alexandria Docks, Liverpool. George was in charge of a maintenance party from 837 Squadron. He had difficulty in finding space for the Fleet Air Arm spares due to the situation on board being one of complete overcrowding of the ship's personnel and the workforce involved in repairs, modification and refit work.

On completion of repairs and modifications *Dasher* moved into the Irish Sea where 837 Squadron landed-on. When sea trials were complete, deck landing practice took place without incident.

As the ship entered the Clyde, 837 Squadron departed for the Royal Air Station at Machrahanish. On coming to anchorage at Greenock, at 5am on 2nd February 1943, George was informed by messenger that he and his maintenance party could leave in a boat which was alongside, if they could board it within twenty minutes, with all their gear. George recalls that he and his maintenance party never moved so fast in all of their lives, but they made it.

Petty Officer Brian A Philpott joined *Dasher* on 22nd January,

1943 at Liverpool. His very first landing on the ship was on 4th February 1943 in a Swordfish. Sub Lt Luke was the pilot. The flight had been of a duration of one and a half hours. Brian knew that the flight deck was a mere 410 feet (120 metres). He was conscious of the need for a good approach if a safe landing was to be achieved. Although Sub Lt Luke was not Brian's regular pilot, Brian considered him a careful and charming man. Sub Lt Luke landed on *Dasher*, as light as a feather. Sub Lt Luke later lost his life whilst flying as a passenger in another aircraft. Brian relates,

> 'On returning to the UK from Iceland, my squadron was moved ashore to the Royal Naval Air Station at Hatson in the Orkney Isles. By the luck of the draw our place was taken by 816 and 891 Squadron, most of whom perished on 27th March 1943.
>
> *Dasher* never really 'shook down' and her reputation as a rogue ship, from the time she was taken over by the Royal Navy, continued until her sad and unfortunate end. In 837 Squadron, our hearts went out to our good comrades in 816 and 891 Squadrons.'

After Operation Torch, when *Dasher* arrived safely at Liverpool, Coder Andrew Cockle left the ship to attend a training course before joining the staff of the Senior British Naval Officers (SBNO) at Murmansk, Russia. Andrew relates,

> 'My memory of *Dasher* is of a spacious and generally comfortable ship, whose ship's company had not really shaken down together to form an efficient fighting unit. I enjoyed my time aboard as much as was possible in wartime.
>
> A great deal of that enjoyment came from the friendship of my fellow members of the communications department and it was a great shock to me to learn of *Dasher*'s demise in which so many of these good friends and comrades were lost. I was so fortunate.'

Fleet Air Arm personnel pictured at Macrihanish. Jack Varcoe (Asst Steward) (10th from left, middle row) perished on HMS Dasher *with many of those photographed. 891 Squadron was in fact disbanded because there were so few survivors*

On February 5th 1943, aircraft number NF684 crashed and was damaged whilst landing on *Dasher*. During 22nd and 27th March 1943, flights of 891 Squadron joined the aircraft carrier. On 23rd March, aircraft number DK 770 was damaged when landing on the ship. The arrester hook rebounded into the plane. On 25th March, when Aircraft HS 230 landed on the flight deck, the arrester hook was pulled out and the aircraft was damaged.

891 Squadron suffered such a high loss of life on 27th March 1943. It was disbanded nine days later, on 5th April, 1943.

Ten months after the disaster, aircraft number NF684 which was damaged during deck landing training on 5th February 1943, crashed into a hillside in north Ayrshire on January 17th 1944, fatally injuring the pilot.

CHAPTER 17

IN MEMORIAM

What can be reasonably concluded about what happened to HMS *Dasher*? Can any reliable cause be affirmed as the likely reason for the loss of a ship and 379 young lives? What can be concluded about the way the disaster was handled by the authorities and has this helped or hindered the survivors to come to terms with a traumatic experience? Was there a cover up? What was the reason that bodies were buried in secret?

The truth is that at this distance in time, the truth will likely never fully be known. It seems reasonable to conclude though, that on the basis of the considerable number of witness statements and documentary evidence compiled within this book, a number of assertions and conclusions can be made. Because of the thinness and the contradictory nature of much of the evidence, they are made not with an air of finality. They are made also, in the face of the loss of so much human life within living memory, in a spirit of humble remembrance for the dead, sympathy for the bereaved and of comfort for the survivors.

The Ship
To convert a cargo vessel into an aircraft carrier within three months is a remarkable achievement. The question arises however, whether at such speed the work had been carried out to adequate standards

of performance and safety. It would appear the speed of the conversion was the most important factor in an attempt to comply with the deadline imposed by the Americans.

When *Dasher* was handed over to the Royal Navy the ship suffered from persistent machinery defects. This caused the aircraft carrier to miss her planned sailing with a convoy departing for the UK on August 1st 1942. Instead, the ship was taken to the US Navy Shipyard, Brooklyn, where an attempt was made to rectify the engine problems.

Dasher was to suffer many further machinery defects throughout her short seven month career. Originally designed and built as a cargo vessel in Pennsylvania, hastily converted at a civilian shipyard in Brooklyn and repaired in the US Navy Shipyard, Brooklyn, on arrival in the Clyde, *Dasher* entered her fourth shipyard where modifications were carried out to the fuel storage and magazines to meet Royal Navy standards. On passage to Oran, for the invasion of North Africa, she suffered further machinery defects and had them rectified at Gibraltar.

On her return to Britain, *Dasher* entered Alexandria Docks, Liverpool for repairs to her main engines. After being forced to leave the Murmansk-bound convoy, due to the American welding splitting apart, she put into Akureyri, Iceland. Her next port of call was the Caledon Shipyard, Dundee, to have her hull repaired. This made a total of six ship yards visited by the aircraft carrier in six months.

It seems clear from witness and survivor statements that many of *Dasher's* crew were far from happy with the experience of sailing her. She was a ship that did not inspire confidence. Without wishing to appear to deny the wartime imperatives that prevailed – these carriers were needed and needed fast – in her quick conversion and multiple mechanical and nautical deficiencies, *Dasher* seemed to be a far from ideal vessel for her purpose. The cracking of welding on her hull on the voyage to Murmansk, by wartime or any other standards, verged on the criminally negligent.

Carley Rafts

When *Dasher* experienced the dreadful storm on the way to Murmansk, the aircraft on the flight deck were lashed down to make them more secure. Everything else on the flight deck that was in danger of being washed away was also lashed down, including the Carley rafts.

This presented very serious problems on 27th March 1943. When the crew were attempting to release the rafts, they could not do so because they were still lashed down. Trying to release them was taking up so much valuable time, the crew gave up and jumped overboard. The few Carley rafts that were released had to have their lashings cut. Fortunately George Lovegrove and one or two other crew members were each carrying a pocket knife.

At the board of enquiry, the captain of one of the rescue ships was asked, 'How many Carley rafts did you see?' He replied, 'Two.' No further questions were asked regarding why so few Carley rafts were in the water, as the enquiry was concerned only with the loss of the ship.

The Cause of the Disaster

Very many witnesses to disasters take a view which explains events, quite naturally, on the basis of the evidence available. If you saw planes landing on an aircraft carrier, you may even have harboured unconscious thoughts as to the danger involved in such an exercise. If, the next thing you see is that aircraft carrier explode and then burst into flames, you may naturally interpret what you have seen as an aircraft crash. You may even be right.

Whatever the cause of the *Dasher* sinking, the cause had to be dramatic and very violent. It is actually very difficult to sink a vessel of her size within the eight minutes recorded by the official board of enquiry. Set her on fire, disable the vessel, cause her to list and then slowly take in water and eventually within some hours, sink – yes. But to sink a ship within such a short time requires major holing of the hull.

We take the view that a crash by one of the ship's tiny Hurricane or Swordfish aircraft, on its own, could not achieve this. It is our view that in order to sink Dasher so quickly a major internal or external assault was necessary.

Since independent witnesses have declared that the aviation fuel storage was not damaged in the initial explosions – indeed the igniting of this and the diesel oil on the surface of the water after the sinking was what claimed so many lives – the events point to a missile or bomb from the outside of the ship or from within. It may never be known whether Dasher was the victim of a 'friendly fire' incident. Submarines were in the Clyde and an accidental firing could have happened.

An examination of the hull of the wreck on the sea bed just could shed some light on this theory. A torpedo strike on the ship would have caused the ship's plates to be blown inwards. An explosive device planted on board would have caused the plates to be blown in an outward direction. Underwater photographs just could resolve what happened to HMS *Dasher*. Although the Hydrographic Office at Taunton have carried out eight underwater surveys of *Dasher*, their findings have never been made public.

The effects of a bomb having exploded on board might also be visible from a hull inspection. Certainly, *Dasher* would have been a useful sabotage target by the Germans and the evidence of the ship's navigating officer presented in Chapter 11 shows that the opportunity for planting a delayed action device was all too available. By today's standards dockside security seemed to be tragically lax.

A Decent Burial

The trouble though, with assessing events surrounding this catastrophe, is that in every respect, today's standards do not apply. The mind of wartime Britain is, for better or worse, remote from the way people think today. Adherence and loyalty to the flag, to King and country, obedience to orders, and a general acceptance of a common set of beliefs just do not apply.

It seems clear from the numerous statements that we have taken that most if not all sailors, airmen, auxiliaries, witnesses and members of the public believed in what they were doing in 1943. There was great unanimity of view. If the authorities ordered that no one should speak about the terrible events, then that was for good reason. To have disobeyed, would have been regarded as letting the side down.

The authorities decided to call a halt to funerals and to public burials after a short time. Bodies, as has been confirmed in official documents of the time, were being washed up on Ayrshire beaches. It appears – again confirmed by contemporary documents – that bodies were disposed of quietly, probably in a plot in Ardrossan cemetery. It seems incredible to us living in the 2000s that relatives would have been denied at least the comfort of knowing finally the fate of their loved ones and that their remains had been laid to rest. An appropriate, if belated, gesture that might even now be considered is the placing of a memorial stone in Ardrossan cemetery to those poor unfortunates who died so tragically and who were denied a public burial.

Security

The sinking of HMS *Dasher* was proclaimed a wartime secret to conceal the loss of the ship from the enemy. Research into German Naval Intelligence records show that the loss of the aircraft carrier was no secret to them.

They were advised of the sinking within days by their agents in Ardrossan and the surrounding area. The Germans could have claimed responsibility for propaganda purposes but chose not to. They preferred to enjoy any benefits arising from the two Allied powers laying the blame on each other.

Bereaved Families

The fact that the ship had been lost was also hidden from the families of the dead. They were led to believe that their loved one had been lost at sea and they have never officially been told otherwise. With the passing of more than half a century, still no official information has been given to the families of the deceased.

The following letter, one message among many similar, from relatives, was written in response to the previous edition of this book. It is from Wilf Scragg of Gwynedd, Wales, the brother of

Francis H Scragg, Acting Air Artificer, Fleet Air Arm who went down with *Dasher*.

Wilf Scragg could be fairly said to sum up the feelings of bereaved families.

> 'When HMS *Dasher* was lost on 27th March 1943, the disaster was immediately shrouded in a blanket of secrecy. Survivors, when they were sent on leave, were instructed not to tell anyone, as were the crews of rescue boats who picked up survivors. It is quite understandable that the British Government would not wish the news of the disaster to be made public during wartime, thus aiding the enemy. It is also safe to assume that German intelligence would have known very quickly of the loss of a British aircraft carrier.
>
> 'After the war, my parents, and I am sure all the other families who had lost loved ones, were expecting details of how and where HMS *Dasher* had been lost, to be revealed. But no, year after year passed by. My mother died in 1956 and my father, an old soldier who lost an arm in France in 1918, died in 1965, with no knowledge of where and how their son had died.
>
> 'Due to the age factor nearly all the parents of the men who died aboard HMS *Dasher* never lived to know what happened to their sons. I find this absolutely deplorable and those in government responsible for such secret laws should hang their heads in shame.'

On Saturday 30th March 1996 a small group who had a shared sorrow, met together at Ardrossan harbour to board the morning ferry across to the Isle of Arran. The group comprised two survivors of the *Dasher* sinking, Fred Plank and Bob Dotchin, Leading Wren Barbara Kay who had nursed the survivors, Wilf Scragg and his son Ken, Arthur Roberts and his wife Ellen, and Stella Cumner. Wilf, Arthur and Stella had all lost a brother.

It was a very poignant voyage for all concerned as they asked each other quietly, 'Who did *you* lose?'

During the voyage Arthur Roberts made himself known to Captain Ian Riggs and explained that they had flowers to throw overboard as near as possible to where *Dasher* lies and would the captain be kind enough to let them know when they reached that point.

Captain Riggs said that on the return journey he would make a small detour to take his ship over *Dasher*. He announced over the loudspeakers that he was stopping the ship for two minutes as a mark of respect and explained why.

When the ship came to a standstill the sea was perfectly calm. It was a tearful moment as two red roses were thrown into the water. As they all stood in silence with their own thoughts and memories, the roses swirled together and disappeared into the depths.

The present HMS Dasher *leads sister vessels* Puncher *and* Archer *to the site of the* Dasher *wreck in the Firth of Clyde for the at-sea memorial service on 5 July 1997 held with survivors from 1943*

CHAPTER 18

THE SECRETS OF THE WRECK
– DIVES ON HMS *DASHER*

HMS *Dasher* is still lying upright on the seabed. She has lain undisturbed protected by the depth of the water covering her. Too deep, out of reach of sport divers.

It came to the authors' attention that the ship had been dived on during 1982; ten years after the dive had taken place. A chance remark by a local taxi driver of how ten years previously he had a regular run to convey Royal Navy divers between the Royal Navy Shore Base, Fairlie, eight miles north of Ardrossan, to a local hotel.

On one occasion one of his regular passengers had a heavily bandaged hand. When the taxi driver enquired about the injury the naval diver answered that while examining HMS *Dasher* he had caught his hand on one of the flight deck arrester wires.

After receiving this belated information contact was made with the Ministry of Defence in an attempt to procure a copy of the dive report. The MOD replied that the report was subject to 30 year's secrecy and they would forward a copy of the report to us in the year 2012. After many enquiries to various departments within the MOD we were advised us that the dive was at the request of the Hydrographic Office, Somerset.

The Officer in Command of the dive vessel, Lieutenant Duncan

Bridge, Mine Warfare and Clearance Officer submitted the following report to the Commander in Chief, Fleet:

> Of the two wrecks examined the Hydrographer was unsure which was the wreck of the aircraft carrier HMS *Dasher*, sunk by a petrol explosion in 1943.
>
> Diving on the wreck of HMS *Dasher* took place on 23rd January 1982 at 2200 hours and was completed at 0535 hours on the 24th January. As a result it can now be confirmed that:
>
> A/ Wreck Number 06300194 in position 55 37 54 North 004 56 53W is that of a fast decomposing trawler or coaster lying on its side.
>
> B/ Wreck number 06201489, in position 55 37 37 North. 005 00 49 West is that of HMS *Dasher*, lying perfectly upright in 170 metres with her flight deck perfectly intact.

Having received confirmation, the dive to examine the aircraft carrier was merely an identification dive, the question has to be asked, why then is the dive report subject to 30 years' secrecy? The dive on *Dasher* then took place in 1982; followed by another survey on 17th April 1984. Yet another survey was carried out on 13th May 1985. Why would it be deemed necessary to carry out all these surveys? Six different sonar scans and a deep dive, all carried out by Royal Navy personnel is quite remarkable. Why so much interest in HMS *Dasher*?

Lieutenant Bridge confirmed that his dive team were officially known as Naval Party Dive Team 1007. The underwater survey on HMS *Dasher* commenced at 10pm on the 23rd January 1982, when three naval lieutenants entered the dive bell. All three men were highly experienced Royal Navy divers. The dive bell was lowered carefully over the side of the MV *Seaforth Clansman* and began its descent while being monitored via the underwater TV system by Lieutenant Bridge on the dive vessel.

As the dive bell pushed past the 100 metres mark the divers were seen to stand up and shake hands. When the dive bell dropped into position on the flight deck the divers connected the speaking system to their 30 metre umbilical cord before leaving the bell and entering the cold water at a depth of 140 metres.

Lieutenant Phil Hammond, the diver who injured his hand, was at his full length of umbilical cord while the *Seaforth Clansman* inched up on her mooring, moving the bell. He noted there was at least one aircraft still on the flight deck. The diver was unsure if he was heading towards the stern or the bow until he came across the aircraft lift shaft on the flight deck. He dropped down into the lift shaft and by torchlight he could see the mangled wreckage of *Dasher's* aircraft. He made no further venture towards the hanger deck due to the danger of becoming tangled in bent-up propellers, engine parts and pieces of fuselage.

The divers had completed their task of identifying the ship and no further attempt was made to dive around the hull. On returning to the bell and being slowly raised to the surface it was noted the dive had taken taken seven hours 35 minutes to complete.

On 29 June 2000 a dive took place on HMS *Dasher*. The planning for the dive commenced in 1998 in Kirkwall, Orkney when members of the European Technical Dive Centre (ETDC) discussed the possibility of being involved in the deepest cold-water dive in Europe. A second planning session took place in Ardrossan, at the home of the authors. The dive team were confident that a safe dive, to lay a memorial plaque on the flight deck, could be accomplished. An assurance was given that HMS *Dasher* would not be disturbed or interfered with in any way. Only one diver would lay the plaque as a mark of respect to the many who lost their lives on the ship.

It was decided the memorial plaque should be A4 size, solid brass and engraved deeply with the words,

DEDICATED TO THE MEMORY OF THE 379 MEN WHO
PERISHED WHEN HMS *DASHER* BLEW UP AND SANK
ON 27TH MARCH 1943

Two days before the plaque-laying the ETDC team arrived in Ardrossan on board one of the three company vessels, MV *Loyal*

Mediator with skipper Neil White. This diving research vessel has a 3000 mile range and a multi-man recompression chamber.

The following day a plaque dedication service was held at Ardrossan Harbour aboard the *Loyal Mediator*. The minister officiating at the service was the Reverend Jim Smith of the local EU Church. After the dedication service a short piece of rope, which had been expertly spliced by Neil the skipper was tied through the two holes that had been carefully drilled. The plaque was now ready and left on board.

The next morning saw clear blue skies and a flat calm sea. After breakfast the mooring ropes were cast off and during the one-hour voyage the dive team sat quietly preparing for the dive ahead. All aspects of the diving procedures were thought over, nothing was left to chance. The team consisted of Mark Reeves, bottom diver; Gary Allison, bottom diver; Alex Deas, deep standby diver; and Tim Claridge, safety diver.

Every piece of dive equipment was checked and rechecked by Alex and Tim. Meanwhile Mark and Gary methodically assembled, checked and rechecked their gas equipment. One last check was meticulously made on the computerised decompression tables before they were laminated. The skipper, Neil was carefully inching the *Loyal Mediator* above HMS *Dasher*. His calculation had to be exact. At the right moment he gave the command to drop the shot-line (a 140-metre length of stout rope with a heavy weight attached). A buoy fixed at the other end marked where the dive was to take place. By viewing the side-scan-monitor the shot-line could be watched dropping rapidly before landing on the starboard side of the flight deck at a depth of 132 metres.

Everyone onboard was playing their part. A trapeze was slung overboard a short distance from the shot line. This is a critical piece of equipment resembling a huge coat hanger. It consisted of a length of scaffolding pole with five air bottles attached plus isotonic drinks. The trapeze was lowered to 18 metres and held in place by two large buoys.

With everything now in place Mark began donning his diving equipment. On completion he strapped on seven heavy bottles. Four contained oxygen and three contained helium. The first diver was ready; the atmosphere was very tense as Mark struggled to his feet whilst bearing the great weight of the seven gas bottles. Holding firmly onto the plaque he edged his way to the side exit of the vessel and stepped off. He disappeared into the sea causing an enormous upheaval of spray and bubbles. On surfacing he swam slowly over to the shot-line and dropped out of sight below the surface. With the shot-line guiding him Mark controlled his descent down to 70 metres passing shoals of stinging jellyfish of different sizes.

Unexpectedly the memorial plaque started to cause problems. It began to swing like a pendulum on a clock. Mark quickly grabbed hold of it before it caused damage to his rubber air tubes. Problem resolved the diver concentrated once more on his descent. With the torchlight struggling to cut through the darkness he checked his depth gauge. It was at 120 metres. A quick look at his watch let him know that four minutes had passed since he entered the water. Suddenly he saw the flight deck and slowed his rate of descent. Touch down – he was standing on the flight deck.

Mark stood for a moment, perfectly still. The only noise was of his own breathing. He checked his computer, 127 metres. On taking a few paces the fine sediment started to rise. On reaching down and putting his hand into it the consistency was like fine clay, four inches (100mm) thick and very easily disturbed. He could feel the hard structure of the flight deck. The disturbed iron oxide filtered through the torchlight.

Mark clipped himself onto the shot-line and moved slowly looking for a suitable place to hang the memorial plaque. There was a considerable amount of netting fouling the superstructure.

He had very little time to spend on the flight deck but the sheer size of the aircraft carrier and the stillness of the water convinced him that if he laid the plaque on the flight deck it would never move. (The Clyde is of course tidal but there is low tidal movement at the Dasher site.)

Mark slowly placed the plaque on the flight deck. As he did so he said to himself all the words engraved on the plaque.

Peering through the gloom – visibility was 3 metres (10feet) –

*Diver Mark Reeves
prior to laying the
commemorative
plaque on the deck of
the wreck of HMS*
Dasher *in June
2000*

the diver could almost see the faces of all the young lads who had lost their lives. The picture of them in *Dasher*'s mess deck enjoying their lunch came to his mind.

His thoughts turned to his wife Sue and two year old son Sam. Mark was at 131 metres. He had been there for ten minutes and the water temperature was 5° Centigrade.

He decided it was time to begin his ascent. To ensure his safety he would have to make a total of seventeen decompression stops varying from one minute to seventeen minutes. The first stop for one minute was only one metre above the flight deck.

On completing most of the decompression stops Mark watched out for the trapeze and made his way over to it. He was now clear of the shot line but within distance to see it. A few minutes after he reached the trapeze he saw Gary descending, with perfect timing, past the very spot Mark had just left. Gary had a total of eight gas bottles strapped onto his back and around his body. Three torches were fixed to a head strap; each torch was shining through the gloom. Mark watched the strong beam of light disappearing as Gary dropped deeper and deeper.

After a five-minute stop Mark continued on his upward journey until he was only six metres from the surface. This was his last decompression stop; he had to remain here for 82 minutes. During this period Alex who was using a Buddy Inspiration Re-breather and Tim who was using a 36% Nitrox twin set continually accompanied Mark.

For the next hour and ten minutes they watched a curtain of bubbles rise from the depths. Finally they saw Gary ascending from the deep and before long he was beside them. One hundred and eighty eight minutes after entering the water Mark surfaced triumphantly and was helped onboard the *Loyal Mediator*.

The whole dive had been executed to perfection exactly as planned. The small team of dedicated professionals had overcome countless obstacles. The hazard of cold, low visibility and extreme depth had been overcome to lay a memorial plaque on HMS *Dasher*.

After the divers had fully rested two minutes silence was observed. Flowers were laid on the water in memory of those who lost their lives and those who grieved. Slowly the *Loyal Mediator* made her way back to Ardrossan.

The next dive on Dasher took place during September 2000. The Northern Gas Team comprising of fourteen divers from the north of England, travelled up to the Clyde with carefully rehearsed plans to complete a dive and photograph *Dasher* on the sea bed.

This dive had been mulled over for a few years and now with closed circuit technology the dive could be accomplished safely. Permission was granted from the Ministry of Defence and the dive was planned to alleviate any concerns that some people might have about the sensitive nature of diving the wreck. The Northern Gas Team's many years experience was to prove invaluable when structuring the dive plan.

Very many lives had been lost when the aircraft carrier exploded and sank. Assurances were given that *Dasher* would be treated with respect and would not be entered or interfered with. The divers would visit the site of the tragic incident to pay remembrance to HMS *Dasher*.

The dive vessel used for the *Dasher* expedition was chartered from Clyde Diving Centre, Inverkip. Jim Queen's 67 feet (20 metres) MV *Spinaway Isles* proved to be an ideal choice with its five heated cabins and a spacious modern shower. The comfort on board was much appreciated as the weather proved to be unfavourable throughout. The dive vessel set off from Inverkip Marina at 8am on 21 September. On reaching the site two hours later diving was postponed due to the deterioration in weather conditions. However they did plot *Dasher* lying at a steep angle on the seabed, the difference in depth being 35 metres between the bow and the stern

The following day weather conditions showed some improvement and again the team set off at 8am.

The first team comprised of Professional Diver Ziad Al-Obaidi. Professional Fire Fighter Ric Waring, Salesman Mark Elliot and Richard Stevenson a technical diving instructor. Richard was carrying a Nikonos 4 camera. It was his job to try to photograph parts of the aircraft carrier.

Ziad was first to reach the fight deck taking just under five minutes. On landing he made his way upwards to the bow reaching the top of the ship at 137 metres. When Richard landed-on he could see the furrow on the mud that Ziad had ploughed as he made his way to the bow. On glancing at his depth gauge Richard noted he was at 141 metres. When he saw a broken and twisted porthole he lined up the camera to take a photograph, however the camera had imploded and was fit for nothing. Minutes later Mark and Ric arrived and stayed low on the wreck at 142 metres.

When it was time for Richard to leave he wished the team luck and commenced his two hour decompression journey to the surface. During his ascent movement on the shot line indicated, with perfect timing, that the second team of four divers were descending. They were Phil Cheetham, a garage owner; designer Tony Harris and finance director Mike Langbourg. As each diver approached Richard moved away slightly from the shot line to allow him to pass.

His two fellow divers Ziad and Ric amassed a total of eighteen minutes on the wreck and explored a considerable distance during which they saw two deck vents and a few blown apart portholes.

The second team headed for the stern and swam alongside the wreck.

Soon all the divers were ascending up the shot line stopping at short pre-planned intervals to decompress. The seven support divers Pete Booth, Lesley Bates, Paul McLean, Ron Mahoney, Simon Townsend, John Womack and Paul Womack were actively swimming amongst the two teams. Two hours later they were all on board enjoying the satisfaction of having safely completed the dive.

Richard Stevenson, the organiser of the expedition summed up his feelings;

> 'HMS *Dasher* brought the group together in late 1995 and it was nice to finally get the chance to explore the wreck, but I don't feel the urge to return. We also proved to ourselves that we could put 8 self-sufficient close circuit divers into deep water, decompress safely and most importantly operate as a team.'

The dive team complied completely with the Ministry of Defence guidelines on property, landing, human remains, photography and munitions.

CHAPTER 19

THE SECRET OF
THE MAN WHO NEVER WAS

October 1942

After the successful invasion of North Africa, in which HMS *Dasher* took part, it became imperative that the allied forces should penetrate into Europe. The island of Sicily, being the closest part of Europe to North Africa, was the most obvious point of invasion.

The British Prime Minister Winston Churchill declared, 'Only a fool would not know where the next invasion will take place.' The German military's heavily fortified presence on Sicily ensured that heavy losses of allied troops would be the result of any invasion.

A recently formed Top Secret Military Intelligence inter-service team, 'The Twenty Committee', met to discuss ways of deceiving the enemy into deploying their troops away from Sicily thus leaving the island vulnerable to allied invasion.

Flight Lieutenant Charles Cholmondeley brought before the committee the rudiments of a plan that his fellow committee members considered bizarre. He suggested planting false invasion documents on a dead body and letting it fall into German hands. His plan was to get a body, disguise it as a staff officer, and give him really high level papers which would clearly show an invasion strategy somewhere other than Sicily.

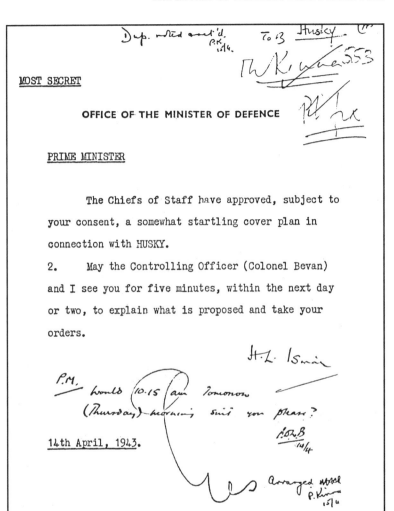

Most Secret memo to Prime Minister Winston Churchill

The Twenty Committee was initially sceptical of the outlandish plan, but the more it was discussed the more it seemed feasible. Flight Lieutenant Charles Cholmondeley and Lieutenant Commander Ewen Montagu took the lead in working out the details of a hoax that would outwit the Germans, gulling them into believing the allies intended to attack the Greek islands, as well as Corsica and Sardinia, not the Italian island of Sicily.

But what about a body and how to get one?

At first it was thought that it would be an easy matter to obtain a body. After all, the country was at war. A telephone call to the Recorder of War Casualties indicated 523 casualties had been recorded for the month of November 1942. It was decided to make a discreet approach to London coroner, Mr Bentley Purchase requesting he locate a suitable body, which had to be undamaged.

The committee's confidence in Bentley Purchase was quickly rewarded. He located the body of a tramp, a down-and-out, who had died after drinking rat poison. To confirm beyond doubt that the body was suitable, advice was sought from Sir Bernard Spilsbury, an eminent forensic pathologist. After receiving confirmation from Sir Bernard the body was then put into cold storage in Hackney mortuary.

It was essential the plan had a code name. Montagu studied the list of code names available from the Admiralty. One of the names appealed to his sense of humour and that was the one he chose. The code name was mincemeat. Now that Operation Mincemeat was official a plan of action had to be worked out in minute detail.

A new identity had to be created for the body held in cold storage. It was agreed by the Twenty Committee to invent 'Major William Martin. Royal Marine' as the courier who would drown while carrying the Top Secret documents.

During the following months the Twenty Committee met on a very regular basis and often their discussions lasted into the small hours. Nothing could be left to chance. One flaw in the deceit would jeopardise the whole operation

Initially they discussed dropping Major Martin into the sea from an aircraft. This suggestion was discounted, as the body could be damaged when hitting the water. A damaged body might appear to be inconsistent with drowning. It was important that the body should be of an officer who had drowned. A Royal Navy submarine was the answer; it could surface undetected close to land. Major Martin could then be lowered from the open deck of the submarine into the water, consistent with accidental drowning. If the tide were calculated correctly he would be washed ashore at a pre-arranged location. After a great deal of deliberation it was decided the site with the best chance of success was at Huelva in Southern Spain. It was well known in British Intelligence that a German agent was very active in Huelva.

When the tide and current floated Major Martin towards land, it was hoped he would be 'found' by local Spaniards. They would then hand him over to the Huelva town officials. When the story of the body reached the ears of the active German agent, he would be sure to play his part by procuring the briefcase and the contents. The documents would hopefully then be passed on to Berlin.

If the documents were believed to be authentic, Abwehr, Germany's Military Intelligence, headed by Wilhelm Canaries, would believe they had come into the possession of a Top Secret military tactical plan and hopefully order the relocation of thousands of troops and heavy armoured divisions away from Sicily.

Success achieved with Major Martin would ensure thousands of allied lives were not lost at the pending invasion of Sicily.

Operation Mincemeat began with the removal of the body from cold storage to be suitably dressed as a Royal Marine officer. After being fully clothed a Mae-West life jacket was then fitted securely. Around his neck was placed a silver cross on a silver chain. An identity disc was attached to his braces; the disc was engraved with the wording Major W Martin R.M. R/C. It was felt to be imperative that Major Martin must be taken for a Roman Catholic since it was considered unlikely that the Spanish would carry out a proper post mortem on a Roman Catholic. Hopefully only a medical examination would take place before burial.

In the corpse's possession was placed everything a man would normally carry such as loose change, a small bunch of keys, and a box of matches, cigarettes, and letters from his father and his solicitor. To fabricate Major Martin's private life, an Admiralty secretary wrote two very personal letters to him as his fiancée. The final touch was a letter from Lloyds Bank, 731 Lombard Street, London urging prompt payment regarding a £79 overdraft. In his wallet was placed a bill from the Navy and Military Club.

A locked diplomatic bag was chained to Major Martin's wrist. In the bag were the Top Secret documents indicating the invasion would take place on Greek islands. To authenticate the fictitious papers three very important letters were also placed in the briefcase. Two letters were supposedly from Lord Louis Mountbatten, one addressed to General Eisenhower, the other to the Admiral of the Fleet. The third letter was from Lieutenant General Nye to General Alexander, deputy to Eisenhower. Personal papers identified the body as thirty six year old Major William Martin, Royal Marines, Military serial number 148228.

The body was then placed in a tubular airtight container and packed with dry ice. Major Martin was ready to play his part in the deception.

The container was to be loaded on to an unmarked van to begin the long overnight journey from London to Greenock in Scotland. From there the canister was to be taken across the Firth of Clyde to the Holy Loch where the *Seraph*, a Royal Navy submarine was to be waiting. The Officer in Command would be Lieutenant LNA Jewell who, only two weeks previously had been awarded the MBE.

One hour after the body was taken on board, the *Seraph* slipped her moorings to begin her covert operation.

A Dead Man Goes To War

During the early hours of April 30th 1943 the *Seraph* kept watch on Huelva beach as the local fishermen got their nets loaded into their small boats and set off for their usual fishing grounds.

At 4.30am the submarine surfaced silently a mile off shore at low tide. The metal container was opened and the body extracted. A check was made that the briefcase was securely attached. The Mae-West life jacket was inflated. Major Martin was placed in the water and slowly started to drift inshore. This was aided by the swirl from the propellers of the submarine as she headed out to sea. Once the *Seraph* was well clear of land the empty container was then pushed over the side. On showing no sign of submerging it was riddled with bullets from the Vickers gun. Mission accomplished the *Seraph* proceeded unnoticed to Gibraltar.

At 9.30am that same morning, lone fisherman Jose Antonio Rey Maria called out to some other returning boats to come and help

MOST SECRET

From The Commanding Officer, H.M. Submarine "SERAPH".

Date: 30th April, 1943.

To Director of Naval Intelligence.

    Copy to F.O.S.

    (for Lt. Cdr. The Hon. E.E.S. Montagu,R.N.V.R.) personal.

OPERATION MINCEMEAT

Weather: The wind was variable altering between SW and SE, force 2. It was expected that the sea breeze would spring up in the morning, close inshore, as it had on the previous morning in similar conditions.
Sea and swell - 2.0. - Sky overcast with very low clouds - visibility was patchy, 1 to 2 miles - Barometer 1016.

2.Fishing boats: A large number of small fishing boats were working in the bay. The closest was left, about a mile off, and it is not thought that the submarine was observed by them.

3.Operation: The time of 0430 was chosen as being the nearest to Low Water Lisbon, (0731) which would allow the submarine to be well clear by dawn. The Cannister was opened at 0415 and the body extracted. The blanket was opened up and the body examined. The brief case was found to be securely attached. The face was heavily tanned and the whole of the lower half from the eyes down covered with mould. The skin had started to break away on the nose and cheek bones. The body was very high. The Mae West was blown up very hard and no further air was needed. The body was placed in the water at 0430 in a position 148° Portil Pillar 1.3 miles approximately eight cables from the beach and started to drift inshore. This was aided by the wash of the screws going full speed astern. The rubber dinghy was placed in the water blown up and upside down about half a mile further south of this position. The submarine then withdrew to seaward and the cannister, filled with water, and containing the blanket, tapes and also the rubber dinghy's container was pushed over the side in position 36°37'30 North 07°18'00 West in 310 fathoms of water by sounding machine. The container would not at first submerge but after being riddled by fire from Vickers gun and also .455 revolver at very short range was seen to sink.
Signal reporting operation complete was passed at 0715.
A sample of the water close inshore is attached.

           N. L. A. JEWELL.

           Lieutenant-in-Command.

Top Secret memos (this page and over) between Madrid and London 20th April and 2 May 1943 on the organisation of the landing of the 'drowned' officer with the case of documents

```
CONFIDENTIAL          M E S S A G E          021738B May

From N.A. Madrid                                   IN

                                          DATE:  2.5.43
                                          RECD:  0310
_____N.S.C. (OTP) by cable_____
Addressed Admiralty for D.N.I.

          R.O. Huelva reports body identified as Major W.
Martin R.M. card number 148228, has been washed ashore at
Huelva.  Death due to drowning probably 8 to 10 days ago.
Spanish Naval Authorities have possession of papers found.
Consul at Huelva has arranged funeral for noon today.

                    021738B
```

33

```
                              MOST SECRET

To:-  N.A. Madrid (Personal)        IMPORTANT

From:-  D.N.I. (Personal            MOST SECRET




          My 041321. Secret papers probably in black
brief-case. Earliest possible information required
whether this came ashore. If so, it should be
recovered at once. If not included with papers in
your 021738, care should be taken that it does not
get into undesirable hands if it comes ashore later.


               071216.
```

him retrieve a body from the water. The other fishermen did not want to assist and left it to the one man to struggle and pull the heavy body half on to the stern of his small boat before slowly making his way to the beach.

At that time the local fishermen lived on the beach, with their families, in rows of little wooden shacks. As news of the drowned British officer spread the children and people came running to see. One man, Antonio El Rafeno remembers when he was 11 years old seeing the body lying on the sand. He recalls how one side of the man's face was black, as if burned. He also recalls looking with envy at the watch on the officer's wrist, the first watch he had ever seen. The man now owns a busy restaurant on that same stretch of beach.

The marine judge, Pascual del Pobil was sent for. He had to oversee the scene of any fatality that took place at the harbour or surrounding beach area before the body could be moved. After the judge gave permission the corpse was placed on a donkey and taken along the beach to Punta Umbria where it could be transported by *canoa* (small ferry) to Huelva.

Meanwhile the judge had taken possession of the locked briefcase. As he was a friend of Vice Consul FK Haselden in Huelva he took the briefcase to him. The British Vice Consul, however, knew of Operation Mincemeat and could not accept the briefcase. Judge Pascual de Pobil was somewhat surprised to be told by the British Vice Consul the proper procedure was to hand it over to the Spanish authorities.

The German agent was Adolf Clauss, son of the German Consul in Huelva. He was working as an agriculture technician on his farm outside the town close to the sea. But he used this job to cover his activities as the Chief of the Abwehr in the province of Huelva. He was soon on the scene and took note of the contents of the briefcase, replaced them unopened, knowing he had come across something of great importance. The body was then entrusted to the British Vice Consul without mention of the existence of the briefcase, which was already on its way to the Spanish Foreign Ministry in Madrid.

The Vice Consul immediately arranged a post mortem by

Spanish pathologist Eduardo Del Torno at Huelva Mortuary, adjacent to the cemetery. On completion the pathologist certified, 'The man had fallen into the sea whilst still alive and had no bruises, death was due to drowning. This body has been in the sea between 3 and 5 days.'

The next day a funeral service was held for Major Martin in Huelva Cemetery. When the Admiralty in London received the official report that Major Martin had 'drowned' and been buried Lieutenant Commander Ewen Montagu instructed that a headstone was to be erected at the grave, with the inscription:

William Martin
Born 29th March 1907
Died 24th April 1943
Beloved son of John Glyndwyr Martin
and the late
Antonia Martin of Cardiff, Wales
R.I.P.

So far all had gone according to plan. Major Martin had carried out his mission and was now buried far from home in a Spanish grave. The Twenty Committee could only wait anxiously to see if Hitler's High Command had fallen for the deceit.

The answer was forthcoming within weeks. The Spanish Foreign Office in Madrid had acted by having the documents opened, copied and resealed before handing them back to the British Vice Consul. The Spanish Foreign Minister Senior Jordana regarded the information as absolutely reliable.

After carefully studying the documents contained in Major Martin's briefcase German Military Intelligence recorded on 9th May 1943:

On balance thought to be genuine, not a plant.

During the next fifteen days Berlin received nineteen top secret signals. One of them described the action taken by the Spanish to

204

To. N.A. MADRID (Personal.)

From. D.N.I. (Personal). *N.° 878*

SPECIAL ROUTE.

Cypher~~xxxxConfidentialxCodexxx~~
Non~~xConfidentialxCodexxxPlainLanguagex~~ } *Delete as necessary.*

My 181213. Bag arrived.

2.   Suggest unless unusual that a medium priced tombstone should be erected on grave with inscription such as quote William Martin, born 29th March 1907 died 24 repetition 24 April 1943 beloved son of John Glyndwyr repetition Glyndwyr Martin and the late Antonia Martin of Cardiff, Wales. Dulce et decorum est pro patria mori. R.I.P. end quote. Order for this tombstone should be given at once.

3.   If currency restrictions would not make it unusual suggest Consul places wreath now with card marked quote From Father and Pam repetition Pam end quote.

E M Montagu

211630 B   N.I.D.12.

                Ext. 193.

D.N.I. only.

                Approved D.D.N.I.

PASS BY HAND

open, copy and reseal the envelopes. The method used by the Spanish was to dry them with artificial heat, carefully open the envelopes and copy the documents. The original documents were then placed back in the envelopes which were resealed. The envelopes were then placed in salt water for twenty four hours.

Another signal mentioned Moreno Fernandez the Spanish Navy Minister, who reported to German intelligence:

Forthcoming allied action in south east Europe.

This information was confirmed when an absolutely trustworthy source, Senor Jordana, the Spanish Foreign Minister reported:

Main attacks would be against Crete and the Peloponnese Islands.

Other signals referred to, 'very trustworthy Spanish sources'. The German ambassador in Rome signalled information from Mr Paolucci, the Italian Ambassador. The signal read:

Based on absolutely trustworthy source, enemy landing in Greece is intended in the next few days.

Having carried out a full investigation and studied the top secret signals, German Military Intelligence issued a report stating:

The authenticity of the captured documents is beyond doubt.

German High Command was also 100% convinced the documents were authentic. When the report reached Hitler, he played his part perfectly. On May 12th, 1943, he issued an order summarising his estimate of the situation in the Mediterranean. The order concluded:

Measures regarding Sardinia and the Peloponnese take precedence over everything else.

Hitler ordered the strengthening of fortifications on Sardinia and Corsica, and he sent an additional *Waffen SS* brigade to Sardinia. He also sent his favourite commander, Field Marshal Erwin Rommel, to Athens to form an army group.

German High Command was aware that the proposed vast amount of troop movement on and around the Greek Islands might very well lead to the Turkish government being very concerned that a German invasion of Turkey was about to take place. The Turkish government was assured by Germany that Greece and the Greek Islands were the objective.

Thousands of German troops, a Panzer tank division, heavy artillery units and Luftwaffe aircraft were all diverted from Sicily when the German High Command ordered the Greek Islands were to be heavily fortified in anticipation of a major allied invasion. Greek Islands that were being defended by Italian troops were bolstered by battalions of Germans.

The Raumboot (R-Boat), armed with six 20 mm anti-aircraft guns was defending Sicily's coastal waters. This lethal, high-speed vessel was also used for mine laying, mine sweeping and escorting U-boats. Such was the success of Major Martin a flotilla of R-Boats was dispersed away from Sicily.

Even more success was to follow, the First German Panzer division was ordered to redirect all their tanks from France, where they were much needed, to the town of Tripolis, 70 miles south of Athens. The German Navy spent valuable time laying three new minefields in Greek coastal waters. Heavy gun batteries were moved to defend the coast of mainland Greece.

Corsica and Sardinia, the other two islands named in the false invasion plans were also heavily fortified by the enemy. The German Navy was ordered to move swiftly in the deployment of fifty extra tanks. Four battalions of infantry with 6 inch and 4 inch guns, anti-tank companies and signal companies were diverted to the islands. German High Command was now confident that any invasion against Corsica and Sardinia would be successfully repelled.

In London, Lieutenant Commander Montagu felt triumphant to receive intelligence reports regarding the enemy's activity. The force of the mighty German army were assembled but in the wrong place waiting for an invasion that would take place elsewhere. The brilliant Ewen Montagu had pulled of a master stroke. Sicily was now undefended against an allied invasion. Operation Mincemeat had been a complete success and would save thousands of lives.

The most fiendish plot ever conceived, was a total success. The corpse of Major William Martin had hoaxed Hitler and changed the course of the War.

On July 10th 1943 British, Canadian and American forces invaded Sicily, under the command of General Eisenhower. 153,000 men swarmed ashore onto the beaches from over 1,100 vessels. The German troops now greatly reduced in number were completely unprepared for invasion and defeated after an intense battle. Allied casualties were classed as light. Operation Mincemeat had been successful.

The details regarding Major Martin were recorded in a file marked Operation Mincemeat. This file was stamped 'Secret for 30 Years' and locked away securely.

In 1951 Ewen Montagu began writing his book *The Man Who Never Was*. This detailed the whole story of Operation Mincemeat and became a bestseller and was made into a feature film starring Clifton Webb. Many people became intrigued as to the true identity of Major Martin. Through the years Montagu's book has been reprinted many times. Researchers have scrutinised the pages searching for clues, trying to ascertain whose body had been used.

In the early months of 1973 the eagerly awaited files were released and placed in the Public Record Office at Kew. Anyone who made the effort to obtain and examine the files were to be disappointed as the papers released did not divulge the true identity of the corpse.

Twenty-three years later, in 1996 Roger Morgan, a local authority planning officer, while researching reports at the Public Record Office, came across papers relating to Operation Mincemeat. The confidential papers had been recently released without any publicity. The documents named Major Martin as Glyndwr Michael, birthplace Aberbargoed, Wales. He was described as being a tramp who had committed suicide by drinking poison in January 1943.

Many newspapers carried articles declaring the name of the person who served his country in the most brilliant deception

A scene from the film The Man Who Never Was *in which Clifton Webb (left) plays Ewen Montagu, here sitting opposite his real life character who had a walk-on part*

operation of World War II. After fifty-three years of total secrecy the identity of Major Martin was at last officially made known.

Now that it was known, it was only right that the correct name should be added to the headstone in Huelva. In 1998, The Commonwealth War Graves Commission contacted the Southern Spanish Branch of the British Legion requesting them to oversee this. That same year a monumental sculptor engraved the following:

Glyndwr Michael served as Major William Martin R.M.

Welsh researcher Colin Gibbon from Pontypridd has been most persistent in his quest to unravel the mystery. For fourteen years he has painstakingly followed up leads in his determination to disclose the true identity of Major Martin.

In the course of his exhaustive research he traced the Commanding Officer of the Royal Navy submarine *Seraph*. Retired Admiral Norman Jewell recalled removing the body from the canister and placing it in the sea. Regarding the body he stated:

'It would be most unlikely that the body of a tramp and a suicide by poison would have been used for the operation.'

The stone marking the grave of the Man Who Never Was at Huelva today. It records the deceased as William Martin and then as Glyndwr Michael. As this book argues the bodies of neither of these men occupy the grave

Another contact he made was with a lady who had been a member of Ewen Montagu's intelligence team. The lady's letter of reply to Colin Gibbon confirmed her involvement with Lieutenant Commander Montagu and Ian Fleming. The letter went on to say that she was still bound by the official Secrets Act, 'however more than one body was used.'

It is recorded that the body obtained in January 1943 was placed in cold storage. On removal, two months later the body would have a fresh appearance but the organs would be mushy. Montagu wrote at the time, 'The organs would be in a very mixed up condition.'

During a post mortem on Major Martin the poison and mushy organs would have been easily detected. If there were any possibility of the Spanish pathologist detecting poison, all would have been lost. The plan would have been doomed to failure resulting in thousands of allied lives lost.

There is no doubt Montagu was in possession of a body before he approached the British War Cabinet. In a letter to his own intelligence team he stated, 'Everything will have to be in place before we seek approval for Operation Mincemeat, otherwise the reply will be: What about this? What about that? Where will you get a body?' Montagu's shrewd legal mind was ensuring approval of his plan.

When the British Prime Minister approved the plan, the intelligence team must have known that the body they already had was of no use for the purpose. The undernourished body of a tramp would bear no resemblance to that of a fit Royal Marine Officer.

Missing Bodies From HMS Dasher

The sinking of HMS *Dasher* in the Clyde estuary on 27th March 1943 resulted in the loss of 379 lives. Only 24 burials were recorded, 255 bodies were never accounted for. Admiralty Office records state,

> 'bodies were being washed up, identified, buried etc on the coast.'

But after eight years of searching cemeteries in the coastal towns of Ayrshire and Inverclyde, the authors found no records regarding other burials relating to HMS *Dasher*.

Telegrams were forwarded to only fourteen families regarding their sad loss and advising that the burials would take place at Ardrossan Cemetery. Four families sent a telegram of reply immediately, requesting their loved ones be buried at their home towns. Three telegram requests were granted. One family who resided in the Scottish Borders was refused.

Another family who resided within twenty miles of Ardrossan desired to bury their son in their home town and travelled to Ardrossan. The father of Sub Lieutenant John McFarlane made his way to the Eglinton Hotel, which had been requisitioned by the Royal Navy. On speaking to the officer in charge of the burials Mr McFarlane requested the release of his son John's body to take him to Greenock for burial. The officer refused. A heated discussion took place between both men. Raised voices were heard by officers in the same lounge who soon made themselves scarce. Under no account would the officer release the body to the family, until the father threatened that he would advise the local newspapers all that he knew about the loss of HMS *Dasher*. Due to the father's determination the body was released to the family.

It seems strange that two families should be refused permission to have their loved one's body released to them. What became of the casualties that were washed ashore? There is no record of burials.

Four days after the loss of HMS *Dasher* on 27th March 1943 Lieutenant Jewell, the Commanding Officer of the submarine *Seraph* was summoned to London to be briefed by Lieutenant Ewan Montagu about Operation Mincemeat. The meeting took place on 31 March 1943. This was the very day twelve of *Dasher's* crew were buried in Ardrossan. By a strange coincidence the orders for Operation Mincemeat were dated 31 March 1943. And Major Martin's Combined Operations Headquarters Pass was stamped Not Valid after 31 March 1943.

At the meeting with Montagu, Jewell was ordered to sail his submarine from Blythe, in the north east coast of England, to the Holy Loch in the Clyde, only eight miles from where *Dasher* sank

Why had the *Seraph* sailed up the east coast of Scotland, round the Pentland Firth then down the west coast to reach the Clyde? During the voyage the submarine sailed past four major Royal Navy establishments before reaching the Clyde. A very long journey to collect a body, which was supposedly being driven north from London, in a van. It seems too much of a coincidence that the *Seraph* should arrive in the area where an aircraft carrier had recently sunk with a great loss of life. Was Montagu delivering a body from London or selecting a new one?

There can be little doubt that HMS *Dasher* provided a rare opportunity to help with the war effort by setting Operation Mincemeat in motion.

Total Secrecy Imposed

On Sunday 28th March 1943, the day after HMS *Dasher* sank, the Royal Navy Press Officer in London contacted the Casualty Section, who was responsible for notifying next of kin. He suggested that telegrams should read:

'Death was due to explosion on board. Ship was in company
with other vessels. Full medical assistance was available
immediately. Everything that could be done to save lives
and mitigate suffering was done.'

379 telegrams were sent out worded as requested.

Six days later the Casualty Section replied to the Royal Navy
Press Office,

'It would be of considerable assistance if any additional
information to supplement the meagre details already given
could be furnished to implement Board decision on casualty
information. Numerous personal calls from distressed
relatives are causing considerable embarrassment to
Casualty Section Staff.'

Three days later the Casualty Section forwarded another letter
drawing attention to the fact that Admiralty policy regarding
information to relatives was not being complied with. They
reminded Admiralty the policy was: As much information as
possible shall be given to next of kin.

The letter went on to say,

Casualty Section Staff are having a difficult time with
relatives on the present meagre information. The ship was
sunk in sight of land, and survivors were picked up by a
merchant ship and landed. It seems that the fate of the ship
must be widely known and that it will not be long before
the enemy hear of it. When can the sinking of Dasher be
released? News of the sinking should be published as soon
as the enemy is found to know or one month from date of
sinking, whichever is earliest.

If this suggestion had been adhered to the relatives of the 379 men
who perished would have been advised of the circumstances on or
before 27th April 1943.

The decision taken was: No information to be announced! The relatives were never told that all information regarding HMS *Dasher* had been made subject to the 30-year secrecy rule.

Two years later, on May 18th 1945 *The Times* carried a small piece subheaded Naval Losses. This listed in minute print the names of ships and the date they were lost not due to enemy action. Contained in the list was *Dasher*, 27 3 43. The actual print size in the newspaper was HMS Dasher 27 3 43.

In 1973 information regarding the sinking of *Dasher* was released to the Public Record Office, Kew. As no announcement was made in the press, the bereaved *Dasher* relatives were never made aware that they could now access information regarding how their loved ones perished. As for the enemy knowing, it is documented, 'We knew within days from our agents and spies.'

Thanks to Welsh researcher Colin Gibbon's persistence with his inquiries the mystery was slowly unravelling. Colin with his wife Heather paid a visit to Huelva to meet with the Spanish researcher Jesus Copeiro who became most intrigued and expressed a desire to become involved.

Jesus Copeiro with his wife Elin next came over to Scotland to meet and talk with Colin and the authors John and Noreen Steele. He also studied the relevant papers at the Public Record Office. Many lengthy meetings took place between the interested parties. Theories were put forward and discounted. John and Noreen Steele journeyed to Huelva to meet with Jesus Copeiro and carry out research in the Spanish town.

The investigation concluded in all parties agreeing with Colin Gibbon's theory that two bodies had been involved in the operation and that Major Martin had been a casualty from HMS *Dasher*.

Colin Gibbon states:

> 'After becoming aware of the sinking of HMS *Dasher* I
> obtained a copy of the book, *They Were Never Told – the*
> *Tragedy of HMS Dasher* and made contact with the authors.
>   'As more details of the secrecy surrounding the sinking
> emerged I became all the more convinced that the body

used for Major Martin had been a casualty from the loss of the aircraft carrier.

'Within days of the sinking of the aircraft carrier Operation Mincemeat was set into action. Why so sudden, the very weekend of the tragedy in the Clyde? Why did Montagu and Cholmondeley arrive at the Port of Greenock, from where bodies from HMS *Dasher* were being brought ashore? They already had the body of a tramp, in cold storage in London since January.

'The meticulous planning certainly paid off when the Spanish pathologist at the Huelva mortuary, who conducted the post mortem on Major Martin, said, "Yes this man drowned at sea and he was alive when he entered the water."

'Operation Mincemeat was risking all and perhaps more importantly thousands of British and American soldiers who would storm the beaches of southern Sicily. No small point could be overlooked and no risk could possibly have been taken, as this would have placed the Germans on a high state of alert. They would have reinforced the obvious beaches and the result would have been another Dieppe, only much worse.

'I have no doubt whatsoever that the body given the identity of Major Martin came from HMS *Dasher*.'

Jesus Copeiro resides in Huelva, Spain. He is a well-known author who specialises in World War II. Mr Copeiro states:

'The planning of Operation Mincemeat was perfect. Major Martin was prepared in every detail with letters, bills, and photos of the fiancée, personal objects and theatre tickets.

'There would not have to be the slightest doubt concerning Major Martin drowning. The body of a tramp that drank poison would not have been used. If it had the Spanish pathologist would have found traces of the poison. Montagu would not have left the slightest doubt concerning the man's drowning otherwise the whole carefully planned and vitally important operation would be ruined so the body had to be that of a person who drowned at sea.

'The Germans must have been completely sure about Major Martin's whole authenticity. So sure that two weeks after the allies had started the invasion of Sicily Hitler still believed the main invasion would take place in Greece.

'As for the true name, the records regarding Major Martin were kept outwith the public domain for fifty years. Some were made available during 1993, 1994 and 1995. However some are still retained, closed to the public.

'I believe the British Ministry of Defence want to hide something serious. Why all the mystery? Operation Mincemeat was not a crime. The idea of complete deception was successful. Why has the case been kept secret, giving only scarce, censored information from time to time? Why wait so long for a simple name of a person. What is hidden? One is obliged to think badly about the way they obtained and prepared the body of Major Martin.

'In 1995, fifty two years after Operation Mincemeat the name Glynwr Michael was released at the Public Record Office. Why has it taken so long for the British authorities to give us the new identity of Major Martin? And having taken so long to give it, why were they in such a hurry to get the name engraved on Major Martin's gravestone?

'For the above reasons, I do not believe that Glynwr Michael could have been the person used for the operation.

'A much more likely theory would have been to use one of the 255 bodies, not accounted for, from HMS *Dasher*. I believe the body was not given to the family; it was kidnapped, to be used in a war operation. Montagu would then have a drowned British body, a perfect body for his plan. All the small details link together.

'I believe the *Seraph* must have travelled to the Holy Loch to fetch the body of a drowned sailor from HMS *Dasher*.'

WM Haggarty BL was a practising solicitor for fifty one years and latterly a consultant with Mathie-Morton Black & Buchanan, Ayr. At Glasgow University he also studied forensic medicine under Professor John Glaister.

Mr Haggarty states,

'I am sure a tramp's body would bear no resemblance to that of an active Royal Marine officer of 36. A competent pathologist would remark on the state of nourishment for example and the state of the liver of an alcoholic.

"When Major Martin was slipped into the water offshore from Huelva the body was found and removed shortly after. Had the body been that of a tramp that had never been previously immersed in water I understand that the lungs would not have contained sufficient water to signify drowning. At the post mortem this is unlikely to have gone unnoticed.

'MoD documents state Major Martin was 36 years of age. The photograph Montagu claimed to be of the body does not look like that of a 36 year old. It looks like the body of a very much older person. The body used was unlikely to be that of a tramp.

'I find it surprising that two Intelligence Officers Lieutenant Commander Montagu and Flight Lieutenant Cholmondeley would travel with a driver overnight in a 3-ton truck to Scotland. A journey, which I recall, was not lightly undertaken in winter even in a motor car at that time.

'It would have been easier for the submarine to have collected the body at Blythe, or any one of the many Naval ports in the south of England.

'Why should the *Seraph* sail all the way up to the north of Scotland, through the Pentland Firth, round Cape Wrath and down the West coast of Scotland to collect a body that has been stored in London?

'The circumstances particularly the time, points to HMS

Dasher. Here they had the pick of the *Dasher* bodies from the Clyde and one closer in age and state of physical condition to Major Martin.

'In view of all the foregoing I consider it very likely that the body used was that of one of the casualties from HMS *Dasher*, although no one can be certain of that until the Navy's records are opened for examination. As for the correct names of the tramp and the body, they must be on record somewhere.

'I am of the opinion that it is very likely the body of Major Martin was that of a *Dasher* victim.'

Herbert Geoffrey Cameron (Geoff) served with the Metropolitan police for thirty years. After serving the initial two year probationary period in the uniform branch he joined the Criminal Investigation Branch (CID), and five years later he was promoted to detective sergeant. During his twenty eight years service with the Criminal Investigation Branch he was attached to the Flying Squad, the Regional Crime Squad, the Organised Crime Squad, the Fraud Squad and other departments. During his police service he was involved in a number of major enquires, the investigation into the activities of the Kray brothers being among them.

In his capacity as officer in charge of a case, like his colleagues who were similarly placed, he had the task of presenting criminal cases before magistrate's courts or crown courts in the London area. On many occasions Detective Sergeant Geoff Cameron found himself presenting criminal cases before His Honour Ewen Montagu QC.

Geoff Cameron states:

'Judge Ewen Montagu was very much feared but highly respected by all court officials, police officers and young barristers. If his Lordship found you wanting I am afraid you got the rough edge of his tongue. You had to be exact, precise and know your particular case inside out, upside down and be prepared for the unexpected question to be thrown at you from him. Failure in any one of these aspects was not to be contemplated. You ignored Ewen Montagu at your peril. To sum up he did not suffer fools gladly.

'As a young detective, at first I was apprehensive of the man, but with time I lost my fear of him and his court because what he was saying was absolutely right and legally very correct. I began to look forward to appearing before Ewen Montagu.

'I saw the mistakes of others and the minefields that exist in a British Criminal Court of Law because of the manner in which Ewen Montagu conducted his court. For me it was a revelation.

'As far as my own career as a detective was concerned I will be forever grateful and I know I speak for hundreds of other detectives who have appeared before him as we all had our knowledge and presentation style enhanced and shaped by this remarkable man. As one of Her Majesty's Judges he was very much respected by the vast majority of CID officers.

'When I retired from the police force in 1991 my wife and I emigrated to southern Spain where I got involved with local radio, initially broadcasting on a discussion programme, which covered all types of newsworthy topics.

'During 1995 the file regarding Operation Mincemeat was released to the Public Record Office in Kew. International newspapers covered the story of Major Martin and it was the subject of one of my discussion broadcasts.

'Over the months and years that followed I probed and asked questions, much as I did as a detective and I have arrived at certain conclusions regarding Operation Mincemeat. To help me in arriving at my conclusions I have communicated with the Prime Minister's Office, the Commonwealth War Graves Commission, Senor Jesus Copeiro, author of the official history *Spies and Neutrals – Huelva during World War II*, the British Consul in Malaga, Jeremy Montagu, son of the Right Honourable Ewen Montagu, the Imperial War Museum and the Ministry of Defence.

'From all these communications, with those persons and organisations and arms of government, as a former trained investigator of crime, I have thought long and hard about all the facts at my disposal. And I am able to arrive at the following conclusions.

'The body of the tramp was kept in Hackney mortuary for an extraordinary length of time. It begs the question – were the planners, in possession of a body which had been damaged by rat poison, deliberately holding it back in reserve in the hope that a better candidate might come along?

'To use the body contaminated with poison was a high risk. Glyndwyr Michael's poison-riddled body was unsafe and does not fit in with the meticulous mind of a trained advocate such as Ewen Montagu. With such high stakes why not use a body that had drowned in salt water? I have always felt uneasy about Glyndwyr Michael's role in this affair and the mere mention of his name raises my eyebrows a notch or two.

'With all the naval establishments on the south coast of England, including submarine depots, why take a body stored in London 500 miles by road, in wartime, to a submarine depot in Scotland. Why not transport the body by aeroplane, or better still, why not by road to a submarine depot in southern England where it could have been loaded onto the same submarine, HMS *Seraph*. Why the Holy Loch in Scotland?

'As for the grave in Huelva cemetery there is a strong school of thought that exists here in Spain that the official war grave of 'Major Martin' is empty and has been since shortly after it was interned there in 1943. Senor Jesus Copeiro propagates the story told to him by the son of the very active enemy agent in Huelva. The agent's son has told Senor Copeiro that the grave was broken into and the body was removed.

'I agree with Senor Copeiro, the body was removed from

the grave. I go further, I say it was removed 3 to 4 days after it was interred.

'Like all other aspects of this remarkable case I came to the conclusion that with documents still booked out to the Prime Minister's Office concerning Operation Mincemeat something pretty remarkable would have to happen, for the complete truth to emerge.

'As for the empty grave at Huelva perhaps a fitting epitaph would be: "Where is The Man Who Never Was"?'

Summary

Operation Mincemeat was the most brilliant deception plan ever carried out during wartime. It was a complete success and saved thousands of allied lives during the invasion of Sicily.

The success of Operation Mincemeat was dependent on Major Martin being accepted as a *bona fide* Royal Marine Officer. Military Intelligence had procured the body of a tramp who had died in January 1943 of rat poisoning. Would this corpse, which was stored frozen in a mortuary pass as a fit Royal Marine Officer who had drowned?

The Commanding Officer of the Royal Navy submarine *Seraph*, Norman Jewell recalled removing the body from the canister and placing it in the sea. Regarding the body he stated, 'It would be most unlikely that the body of a tramp and a suicide by poison would have been used for the operation.' A member of Ewen Montagu's Intelligence Team stated, 'Two bodies had been used in the operation.'

Would it have been possible to procure another body, one more suitable to the task ahead? Did an opportunity present itself when HMS *Dasher* sank in the Firth of Clyde on 27th March 1943 with the loss of 379 lives?

For many days afterwards drowned members of her crew were being washed ashore at Ardrossan. A funeral parade was held in the town on 31st March but only twelve burials took place. On that same day the Officer Commanding the *Seraph* submarine was summoned to a meeting in London with Ewen Montagu. The orders for Operation Mincemeat were signed that very day. Also Major Martin's fictitious pass for Combined Operations Headquarters was stamped 'Expired 31 March 1943.'

The submarine *Seraph* departed from the south east coast of England and proceeded to the Firth of Clyde where HMS *Dasher* had four days previously exploded and sank.

The operation was now underway. A few days later two members of the Twenty Committee, Ewen Montagu and Charles Cholmondeley also made their way to the Clyde with the purpose of handing over the corpse of Major Martin to the now waiting submarine. Had the body of a tramp been placed in the container, which was taken on board the submarine, or had a fresh body now been acquired from HMS *Dasher* for Operation Mincemeat to be set in motion?

Although the body of Major Martin was found within a few hours by a fisherman and removed from the sea at Huelva the Spanish pathologist recorded, 'The body had been in the water between three to five days.'

On the instructions of German Military Intelligence, Major Martin's body was removed from the secluded grave, four days after burial, to allow a skilled German pathologist to carry out a thorough post mortem. This is confirmed by a search in the Public Records Office which found a German document translated by the British Enemy Document Section. The small part of interest here read:

Operation Mincemeat
(Engl. Kurierfund)
    The body was removed 4 days after interment, for the purpose of a post mortem by a German pathologist.
Enemy Documents Section.
25th March 1945

The German pathologist recorded, 'The body had been in the water between five and eight days.' The question remains, which water? Could it have been the Firth of Clyde?

After the post mortem would the Abwehr risk another covert

operation to return the body to the grave? A few days later a heavy slab engraved with the name, Major Martin, was placed on the grave, which in all probability was and remains empty.

In 1951, Ewen Montagu began writing his book concerning Operation Mincemeat. The text of his book had to be passed to the MoD for approval. In the manuscript it was stated about the body used in the operation:

'When it looked as though our plot was going to be stillborn a report came through about an officer of one of the services who had just died of pneumonia in a remote part of the country. Pathologically speaking it looked as though he would answer our requirements. All that I can say here is that the dead officer was in his early 30s.'

It also recorded:

'The right body was found at the right moment.'

It has never been explained why the sinking of HMS *Dasher* with great loss of life was subject to the 30-year secrecy rule. Did the covert use of a seaman's body from HMS *Dasher* create the need for the secrecy? Is this also the reason why the large number of bodies brought ashore and washed ashore were secreted away to unknown graves? Was one of them The Man Who Never Was?

Who Was Major Martin?

Ever since the success of Operation Mincemeat there has been much speculation as to who became Major Martin. Many researchers have dedicated years trying to unravel the mystery. The fact is that the Admiralty intelligence committee realised that the body stored in dry ice was of no use to them as it bore no resemblance to that of a fit Royal Marine officer. Also a post mortem would reveal that Major Martin did not die of drowning.

Lieutenant Commander Ewan Montagu who master minded the operation, recorded:

John Melville pictured with his wife and daughter in March 1943, 15 days before disaster

Very tentatively we opened enquires in service medical circles. It was a very odd question we had to ask. Could we obtain possession of a body whose cause of death could be confused with shock or drowning or injury? The body does not have to be that of an officer but it must look like an officer.

We encountered deep suspicion but we kept on. We received various 'offers' but for one reason or another they were not satisfactory. Finally when it looked as though our plot was likely to be stillborn a report came through about someone of the services who had just died of pneumonia, in a remote part of the country.

Pathologically speaking it looked as though he would answer out requirements.

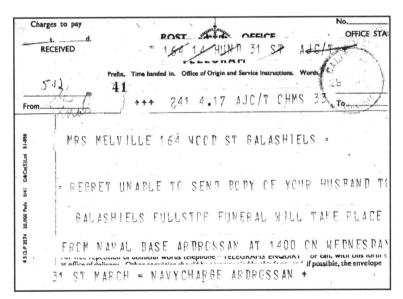

Telegrams sent to John Melville's widow

29th March, 1943.

Dear Madam,

In confirmation of the telegram already sent to you, I deeply regret to have to inform you that your husband, John Melville, (Ordinary Coder, C/JX.361352), has been killed while on war service on 27th March 1943.

Please allow me, on behalf of the officers and men of the Royal Navy, the high traditions of which your husband helped to maintain, to express my sincere sympathy with you in your sad bereavement.

I am, Madam,

Yours sincerely,

Commodore.

It would appear that a member of the services medical circle in Ardrossan responded to the above request by targeting the body of Sub Lieutenant John McFarlane. Why else would a senior Royal Navy officer refuse to release the body to his father? It was only after the grieving father gave vent to his anger and threatened to contact the newspapers that he was grudgingly given permission to take his son home to Greenock for burial.

The following day fifteen families received telegrams advising them that their loved one was being buried in Ardrossan Cemetery on the 31st March 1943. Four of the families responded immediately by forwarding a telegram that it was their wish that their loved one be returned to their home town for burial.

Three of the requests were granted. The young widow of John Melville, who resided in the town of Galashiels in the Scottish Borders, was refused permission. She wanted to have her husband buried where she could visit his grave with her small daughter. This was not to be as she received a telegram stating 'regret unable to send body to Galashiels' and that the funeral would take place in Ardrossan. The young mother was in no state of mind to question authority.

For years the authors have been of the opinion that the evidence strongly pointed to Major Martin being in reality John Melville. While researching the first edition of this book, *The Tragedy of HMS Dasher*, we visited John Melville's daughter Isobel and her husband Kenneth Mackay on more than one occasion. Isobel is very proud of her father and the authors never did voice their belief that his body had been used in the wartime ruse. It was felt that such a disclosure could cause a great deal of upset to the family.

After *The Secrets of HMS Dasher* was published in 2002 the authors received an astonishing phone call from Isobel Mackay. She stated that while she was reading this book in her garden summer house she had a very strong feeling that Major William Martin was her dad. Was this possible?

It seems more than likely that John Melville was chosen. He was a fine looking man in his late 30s, just what Lieutenant Commander Ewan Montagu required. Why else would only this one body be held in Ardrossan and the families request for it denied? Only his keys were returned to his widow and the information that he was recovered near the Holy Isle off Arran, and he would be buried in Ardrossan.

Mrs Mackay finds it a comforting thought that her dad was involved in the saving of many thousands of lives. John Melville lost his own life but he did not die in vain.

HISTORY OF HMS *DASHER*

Archer Class Escort Aircraft Carrier

1941

12 April. Launching of American merchant vessel *Rio de Janeiro*. Built by Sun Shipbuilding & Dry Dock Company. Chester. U.S.A,

22 November. *Rio de Janeiro* taken over by US Navy for conversion as an Archer Class Aircraft Carrier. Given the code letters BAVG-4. Pendant D 37

1 July. Conversion completed at Tenjens & Lang Dry Dock Company. Hoboken. New York. Handed over to US Navy.

2 July. Official hand-over ceremony from US Navy to Royal Navy on lease-lend. Ship named HMS *Dasher*

3 July. Brooklyn Navy Yard.
0900 Engine trials.
1330 both bow anchors dropped.
1430 engine trials complete.

4 July
1130 first aircraft lands.
1241 aircraft crashes whilst landing on deck. Pilot unhurt.
1410 Aircraft attempting to land fails to connect with

arrester wire crashes over bow into sea. Aircraft sinks, pilot picked up by rescue boat unhurt.

5 July / 29 August. Engine trials and defects rectification. Fire broke out on board. Further repairs carried out. HMS *Dasher* prepares for convoy duty.

Armament Taken Onboard
Three single 4 inch American Mark 9 Anti Aircraft Guns
Ten single Oerlekon 20 mm Anti-Aircraft Guns
Three 40 mm Anti-Aircraft Guns
80 Mark 7 Depth Charges
500-pound Semi Armour Piercing Bombs. Anti U-Boat
250-pound Semi Armour Piercing Bombs. Anti U-Boat
250-pound General-Purpose Bombs
68 Torpedoes
Thousands of rounds for Aircraft machine guns
Flares
Pyrotechnics

30 August Sailed in Convoy HX 205 from Hudson River to the Clyde via Halifax, Canada.

11 September. Upper Clyde shipyard. Modifications to Royal Navy standard commenced.

27 October Modifications complete. All dockyard workmen left ship.
1520 slipped mooring. Boom net lowered. Sailed for lower Clyde past Cumbrae.
1710 Swordfish aircraft landed. Pass Pladda and Ailsa Craig. Anchor at Holy Isle.

28 October At Sea
0645 sighted HMS *Argus* & HMS *Jamaica*. Aircraft landed on.

29 October Return to Clyde

30 October In company with HMS *Argus*, HMS *Jamaica*, HMS *Delhi* and 4 escorts. Depart Clyde with convoy Code name

Force LX. Forming part of Eastern Naval Task Force.
Operation Torch. Invasion of North Africa.
1445 HMS *Zetland* makes contact with enemy submarine.
Emergency turn to port. 1448 HMS *Zetland* making depth
charge attack

30 October. At Sea
0845am. Cease zigzag course.

31 October At Sea Convoy bound for Oran, North Africa.
One of six UK convoys. Total ships departed UK, 215.
One US convoy, 'Task force 34', 99 ships. Total number of
ships involved in Operation Torch, 314.

1 November. Pass 5 miles off Lisbon. Aircraft sighted. Identified
as friendly

8 November. Off Oran. North Africa. Action stations. In position
with HMS *Rodney*, HMS *Furious*, HMS *Biter*, HMS *Delhi* and
nine Royal Navy destroyers.
0500 Heavy gunfire bombardment commences from all HM
ships. Return gunfire from Oran. Heavy bombardment
sustained. Dasher receives signal, 'Alter position to receive
protection from guns of HMS *Rodney*.' All aircraft flew off to
provide escorts for bombing raids, secure air cover at Oran
and to drop propaganda leaflets.

9 November. All aircraft flew off.
0600 Enemy submarine contact. HM ship carries out depth
charge attack astern.

10 November. At Sea.
1124 Submarine contact. Emergency turn to port.
1127 Resumed course. Arrive Gibraltar.

11 November 1100 Armistice day observed.
1120 two ratings arrive from HMS *Biter*.

12 November Secure for sea. In escort with convoy MFK1 from
Gibraltar to UK.

November 13. Commence zigzag course. Convoy time advanced one hour.

November 14. 1300 aircraft sighted. Commence zigzag course.
Aircraft friendly. cease zigzag course.
Arrive at Liverpool for repairs and fitting of Air Defence Room. Allocated to Home Fleet.

December. Wrens invited onboard for tea

1943

27 January Depart Liverpool for Clyde.

28 January Arrive at Clyde. Vice-Admiral-Aircraft-Carriers onboard. Flying trials.

29 January Arrive Greenock

January 31 Arrive at Rothesay Bay. Clyde. Depart for Scapa Flow.

February 1 Arrive Scapa Flow for work-up

February. Take part in royal visit. HM King George V1 inspects Fleet. Excess of 200 vessels in Scapa Flow.

15 February Sailed in convoy JW53 bound for Murmansk. Squadrons 816, 837 and 891 onboard. Aircraft, Swordfish & Hurricanes.

17 February Convoy encounters storm force winds, snow squalls and severe icing conditions. Port side lifeboats and Carly floats whipped from their davits and stowage positions. Three swordfish aircraft lashed to flight deck washed overboard. Weather extremely savage. Speed maintained. Dasher suffers from severe weather damage. American welding of hull splits apart. Ship ordered to depart from convoy, proceed to Seydisfiord. North east Iceland.

18 February 9am arrive off Seydisfjiord.

1530 Enter Seydisfjiord in company with HM ships *Belfast*, *Cumberland* and *Soylla*. Dasher at anchor. Review of damage. Refuelled Ship. Proceed to Eyjafjordur, north east Iceland. Anchor at Akureyri. Ship careened-over. Temporary repairs carried out.

Proceed to Caledon Shipyard. Dundee. Permanent repairs took 3 weeks to complete. Sail to Rosyth Royal Navy dry dock. Hull inspected.

Mid March. Proceed to Clyde. Anchor at Tail o' the Bank, Greenock

24 March Commenced work-up in Clyde area.

26 March Boom net lowered at Lamlash Bay. Arran. Enter. Anchor dropped

27 March. Day of The Tragedy.

0900 Depart Lamlash Bay. Involved in aircraft landing exercises. 12 depth charges removed from forward bomb room and 12 removed from after depth charge magazine. Stowed in the port and starboard side of hanger. 12 feet (3 metres) from aircraft lift. All for ready use. 68 depth charges left in depth charge magazine.

Removed from stowage, 9 torpedoes with warheads and primers inserted. Stowed in hanger. 3 on either side of lift well. 3 on a rack port side.

1635 Last signal from Dasher to Lamlash Signal Station, Arran. 'Will arrive Greenock at 1800 hours'.

1640 Dull thud heard throughout ship, not unlike backfire from engine. Followed immediately by horrendous explosion. Many large fires broke out in hanger area. Aircraft machine gun ammunition exploding.

1642 Ship commences to sink at the stern.

1645 Ship's bow rises slowly out of the water almost vertical pointing to the sky.

1648 HMS Dasher sinks stern first to170 metres to rest upright on seabed.

Battle Honours

Atlantic.   North Africa.   Arctic.

Particulars

Overall length. 494 feet. (145 Metres)

Beam. 70 feet. (20 metres)

Speed. 16 knots

Fuel stowage. 75,000 gallons. (337,500 Litres)

Displacement   8,200 tons.

Aircraft. Sea Hurricanes and Swordfish. Between 12 and 16 at any one time.

Catapult. Aircraft catapulted off ship by means of a hook attached to a steel cable driven by compressed air. The cable ran along a 35 metre (100 yard) groove on the flight deck. As hook disengaged it flung the aircraft at high speed off the ship into the air.

GLOSSARY

Aft	From the centre of the ship to the stern
Aircraft lift	A large lift weighing up to 12000lbs (2660kilos). Transported the planes between the flight deck and the hangar.
Arrester hook	A hook fitted at the rear of all aircraft involved in landing on an aircraft carrier. As the aircraft landed, the hook caught one of the arrester wires bringing the plane to an abrupt halt.
Arrester wires	Fitted on the flight deck, up to 5 arrester wires fitted on each aircraft carrier.
Bilges	The lowest internal portion of the hull.
Bow	The front of the ship.
Carley Raft	A light rubber dinghy which could be thrown over board in an emergency.
Crash Stations	Alerting the crew that the ship was about to sail at top speed.
Fleet Air Arm	Personnel attached to aircraft which land on aircraft carriers.
Flight Deck	The flat uppermost deck where the aircraft landed.

Float-a-net	A large rope net with cork discs attached.
Forward	From the centre of the ship to the bow.
HMS	His/Her Majesty's Ship
Hangar	The deck below the flight deck, where the aircraft were stored, maintained and refuelled.
Island	Where the navigation, communication and day to day running of the ship is controlled by the captain and senior officers.
Mess	Crew's eating area
NAAFI	A civilian run canteen/shop. Found in all military establishments. Supplied toiletries, cigarettes, tea, coffee, etc. The name is an abbreviation of Navy, Army, Air Force Institution.
Port	Left hand side when facing the bow.
Sonar scanning	Sonar scanning sends out high pitch sounds to the seabed. The sound waves bounce off a shipwreck back to the scanner where the wreck shows up on the screen.
Starboard	Right hand side when facing the bow.
Stern	The rear of the ship.
WVS	Women's Voluntary Service
Wrens	Women's Royal Naval Services

\